The Cookie Jar and Other Plays

The Cookie Jar
and
Other Plays

by
John Clark Donahue
edited by
Linda Walsh Jenkins

UNIVERSITY OF MINNESOTA PRESS, MINNEAPOLIS

Acknowledgments

The Rockefeller Foundation's support and encouragement of the Children's Theatre Company in the compiling and preparation of these scripts is most gratefully acknowledged. Among the individuals whose assistance and collaboration have been important in making this volume possible are Gerald Drake, Timothy Mason, and Jan Archerd of the Children's Theatre Company; Arlen Snesrud, music copyist; and John and Robert Jenkins.

L. W. J.

Contents

Halftones follow each play.
    Color photographs follow page xx.

Preface

John Donahue describes all his plays for young people and their families as "experimental." By using the word "experimental" he places the plays in a category which implies that their content and form may not necessarily coincide with the audience's preconceptions of what theater for children has to be. While the plays are not experimental in the usual sense of the word (that is, they do not attempt to create new stage spaces or to use innovative performance techniques), in a number of ways they represent a radical departure from the usual theatrical fare for children. None of the plays have moralistic aims such as to teach children how to be good citizens. None follow the traditional academic prescriptions for the writing and staging of plays for children. Those young people and their parents whose theater experience has been limited to the animations and the pseudorealistic family adventure stories on television may not find Donahue's plays easily accessible at first because the messages and symbols are implicitly, not explicitly, communicated, and scenes and images often appear to be fragments of dreams. Instead of using uncomplicated linear plotting Donahue challenges young audiences with flashback, montage, slow motion, and scenes that flow from one to another without breaks — cinematic techniques that have become almost a trademark of Donahue's writing and directing.

Donahue is more interested in introducing young people to mystery than in giving them what is safe and familiar. "The question of methods, disciplines, techniques, and all that stuff that people talk about gives way to a search for beauty and loveliness in one's self. The young minds — the open ones, the ones that still recall the smell of mud in the spring and the way the statue in the park talks at night — will wander in and watch awhile, and if they like the tune well enough, they'll play it on their own harps one way or another, beautiful and lovely." Donahue has intuitively approached theater for children in a way that the Swiss child psychologist Jean Piaget might approve. Piaget suggests that intelligence develops as the child intellectually organizes new stimuli and adapts to them; it follows that if theater for children is to serve intelligence it must offer surprises and challenges to the child's mind and imagination. Donahue and the Children's Theatre Company attempt to provide theatrical stimuli that both educate and entertain. Piaget theorizes also that children have the ability to construct a reality that transcends the mere appearance of things, and it is that transcendent reality that Donahue seeks to evoke in his plays. (The history of the Children's Theatre Company is described in greater detail in *Five Plays from the Children's Theatre Company of Minneapolis,* edited by John Clark Donahue and Linda Walsh Jenkins, University of Minnesota Press, 1975.)

All of the plays contain surrealist elements that are designed to provoke curiosity and to conjure up dream-visions. For example, in the prologue to *How Could You Tell?* the bizarre image of the puppet is meant to trigger dream-consciousness in a child's imagination (the little circus of the mind) as a vantage point from which the child may perceive the rest of the play. Donahue wants his productions to elicit many questions (particularly those to which there are no easy answers) from the children in the audience, and he has faith in the ability of children to grapple earnestly and thoughtfully with such questions. "Children are willing to play games of Chase the Papa Bear in a Zipper Suit around the room and Stamp Your Feet and Count to Ten, but then they retire to some mossy, wet place to wonder when they will die — and then they fly home to eat supper again. And so on it goes, every child getting older and, if he's not careful, stupider, and settling down to live his life. So let us tell all of our stories, whether in paint, or on paper with pen and words, or on the stage, or in light, or out of old rusty pipes, wherever and however, with a driving awareness of the fact that we are human beings. And if we have forgotten what this means, if we are in doubt about how we should behave or react or think or feel, let us be concerned and look to the brilliance of our youthful eyes."

A number of distinctive motifs, images, and themes occur in Donahue's plays. The birds that chatter and flutter in elaborate cages in his own home appear symbolically or literally in his plays. In *How Could You Tell?* Elaine affectionately refers to Emile and Jane as "my little birdies" when they tell her of their desire to escape, to fly away. Many of the images in the plays are based on intense experiences from Donahue's own childhood. The collage of games in *Old Kieg of Malfi* recalls the street games of children in the neighborhood at twilight. Donahue reconstructs his impressions of the curious, foreign-sounding gibberish that adult prattle is to the ears of a child in Old Kieg's Kool-Aid lecture and Eugene's speech as a circus barker. The rituals of friendship and challenge that children act out socially are often part of the dialogue in Donahue's plays; for instance, in all three of the plays in this volume children taunt one another and brag about their exploits. In *The Cookie Jar* the manner in which Bubble and Black-Eyed Pea test each other contrasts with the vicious warring among the teenagers who follow the Stale Cake Company. In all of his plays Donahue invites the audience to share the children's private speculations about subjects as diverse as death and dance lessons.

Music is essential to all of the plays produced by the Children's Theatre Company, partly because it elicits an emotional response that helps the audience to transcend "the mere appearance of things." In addition, it provides the framework for songs and dances, supplies overall form and thematic content in each play, and makes possible flowing transitions from scene to scene. The composer (who usually serves also as an accompanist) attends rehearsals and creates the score as the script evolves. All the mood music, transitions, and musical cues are developed during rehearsal. The composer, working without copying assistance, barely finishes the working score for one show when work must begin on the next. As a result, a complete reading score with all parts represented was never developed for either *Old Kieg of Malfi* or *How Could You Tell?* (Roberta Carlson, the composer and accompanist for the shows, played many portions of her own piano and percussion parts from memory, and therefore she rarely had occasion to write them down.) The examples of the score for *The Cookie Jar* that appear in this volume illustrate the variety of rhythms, moods, and styles that a composer can infuse into a single production.

The task of weaving together the components of plot, action, music, design, and staging usually begins about six weeks before the preview of a show. A production team including Donahue, the designers, and the composer hold several sessions to begin developing a plot outline, design concepts, and musical themes from ideas that have been allowed to simmer since the script was first selected (usually the preceding winter). These ideas are then presented in a production meeting that is open to the entire staff. By this point the set designer has made a scale model which becomes the basis for a "talk through" of the show. The costume designer presents sketches with ideas for styles and colors together with samples of fabrics. Those in charge of promotion for the show select scenic elements and costumes that must be ready for photographing as soon as the show is cast. After the production concepts are approved, the technical director makes working drawings so that carpentry and construction can begin.

Auditions for casting are usually held at about the same time. Those who audition are usually taught a simple song and a short dance pattern; each person practices and performs with a group at first, then alone. Often the young actors are asked to pantomime a situation involving a series of actions: "You enter your room, sit on a chair, and brush your hair. Your dog runs to you and leaps onto your lap. You kiss the dog, put it down, and send it out of the room." Occasionally the actors read or memorize a short speech from the play, and sometimes Donahue invents a speech on the spot for the actors to repeat or to paraphrase. In all cases Donahue looks for certain qualities of voice and physical appearance, aptitude for learning quickly from a director, ability to perform strenuous or complicated physical tasks, stage confidence without arrogance, and a courageous, intelligent, and tasteful approach to acting. A call-back session is held soon after to allow Donahue to give closer attention to the actors who appear to be possible casting choices. In this session the actors are usually placed in improvisational situations that relate to the play (for instance, improvising a circus walk-around for Donahue's *How Could You Tell?*). Actors employed by the theater as well as children, teenagers, and adults from the community audition for each show.

During the two or three weeks of rehearsals after the casting is complete, the characters and the action of the play are sketched out and most of the scenes are blocked and choreographed. Since the setting itself is an integral part of many scenes and dances, these sequences cannot be choreographed until the cast begins to rehearse on the set. The actors rarely carry scripts unless they have very long speeches to learn; usually they take their lines directly from Donahue and are able to retain them after several rehearsals of each scene. Donahue remembers that once a man commented, after observing the rehearsal of a play that included many children in the cast, "My, you don't treat them as children, do you!" Donahue's immediate response was, "No, we don't!" He explained later that this was not exactly true: " 'Yes, we do,' I should have answered, or 'We try to . . .' You would be amazed at how delighted and grateful they are to be shown the way out of childhood . . . a peculiar time reserved for dolly routines and little harness games in the yard, all designed to nurture a simple, mindless raggy bag, capable of doing nothing worth much at all beyond entertaining Grandma a very slight bit on her birthday."

Before the opening of the new theater facility in 1974 the company mounted its current play in the auditorium of the Minneapolis Institute of Arts for performances during the day and conducted rehearsals for the next production in the evening somewhere else (often in a church or a school gymnasium). The set of the show was dismantled and removed from the auditorium only about twelve days before the preview performance of the new one. As soon as the stage was cleared, the basic set for the new play was trucked from the shop several blocks away, hauled into the auditorium, and hurried onstage so that the cast and the crew could begin work.

At this point in the rehearsals the end of the play often was not yet blocked, and sometimes the final scenes were not even sketched out.

(No one, not even Donahue, knew how *How Could You Tell?* would end until the day before the preview.) Meanwhile, the composer was busily writing parts for the orchestra and rehearsing with them (often in "spare" time left over after participation in cast rehearsals, teaching Theatre School classes, and attending staff meetings), costumes were beginning to arrive, and sound tapes recorded during the day were added to the rehearsals that night. About a week before the preview, most of the costumes and stage properties were ready, the actors were beginning to experiment with their makeup, and set painting and decoration were in the final phases. The initial technical rehearsals for lighting and sound crews were usually held less than a week before opening night.

The last five days before the opening were predictably chaotic as the company struggled to fit all the pieces into place and to integrate them into a performance for the preview night audience. Fortunately this audience was made up of families and friends who forgave the inevitable opening night errors. Still, no one in the cast or the orchestra of Donahue's *How Could You Tell?* will forget the preview of the scene in which a raft (an enormous circular platform) on the sea glides slowly downstage to extend slightly past the apron. On the preview night, instead of gliding slowly down the stage the raft scooted rapidly toward the apron, slipped its moorings, and almost plunged off the stage into the midst of the horn players and the audience in the first rows. In the meantime the actors who were huddled on the raft bravely sang "The Song of the Sea" as their craft teetered dangerously. Another unforgettable preview mishap (but not such a hazardous one) occurred during the opening of *Cinderella* in the scene where the coach is supposed to arrive and carry Cinderella off to the ball while her fairy godmother stands waving good-bye in the gently falling snow. But when the time came to unroll the carriage drop (which had been hung only an hour before), a drop of a kitchen unrolled — completely obscuring Cinderella and leaving the godmother onstage waving good-bye through the kitchen window in a flurry of styrofoam snowflakes that made unmistakable "clunks" as they hit the stage floor. The new theater complex, with auxiliary rehearsal rooms and ample space to fly sets, has made it possible for the company to shift to a repertory format which eliminates many of the production problems that were routine during the company's first decade. But preview misfortunes are inevitable under even the best of conditions.

The plays in this volume were created in the theater, scene by scene, during the rehearsal period. (Donahue does not write a script before the rehearsals begin, nor does he ever write stage directions.) These scripts represent a blending of Donahue's imagination with the skills and artistry of the actors, the composer, and the technical staff. Within this stimulating ambience Donahue invents the play and literally directs the script into being. He might begin by asking the composer to create something on the piano that has the particular flavor he wants (for instance, "Dagwood Bumstead in London") while he gives the actors another evocative image (it might be "chickens in a barnyard") on which to elaborate the action of a scene. The actors take their lines from Donahue as in improvisation. He usually sits in the center of the auditorium or stands in the pit at the edge of the stage, sometimes leaping onto the stage to demonstrate a dance step or a certain body posture.

Donahue's approach to playmaking incorporates many elements from his extensive background in painting, music, and poetry. Considered in chronological sequence, his five plays for children reflect his evolution from a painterly director to a playmaker who translates the activities, insights, make-believe, and dreams of childhood into theatrical metaphors. His earliest plays are almost exclusively visual — *Good Morning, Mister Tillie* (produced in 1966 and 1970) is a mime fantasy, and *Hang On to Your Head* (1967, 1972) uses dialogue only sparingly — but a look at the content, plots, and staging of these plays reveals a number of modes of artistic expression which are interwoven in the plays that appear in this volume.

Good Morning, Mister Tillie is about a little man whose balloon is constantly threatened and pursued by the Big Odd-Glasses Man, the manifestation of Mister Tillie's fears. The pursuit progresses in dreamlike fashion through an illogical and highly fanciful assortment of scenes and images in black and white: a sculptor's studio, a wind tunnel, busy Parisian streets, a jungle, a grand ballroom, a ballet studio, and other settings. All the actors are dressed in white with clown-white makeup. The stage floor is black and the sides and back of the stage are hung in black velours. As long as Mister Tillie is pursued by the Big Odd-Glasses Man, there is no color on the stage. A taped score of electronic music and contemporary compositions emphasizes the stark, fear-laden atmosphere. As Mister Tillie gains strength and confidence and becomes aware of the gift of love, he banishes fear — and the orchestra bursts into Vivaldi, the stage fills with color and the babble of voices, and Mister Tillie ascends (presumably to some rarefied stratum) as the people shower him with flowers and confetti.

Mister Tillie's balloon represents the part of his being that he holds most dear — the artist within himself. He is possessed by fears and insecurity, but he finally gains personal strength through love and fear can no longer threaten him. Mister Tillie's fears and nightmares reflect images from Donahue's personal experience and feelings as he created *Good Morning, Mister Tillie,* which was his first play and the first "experimental" play produced by the Children's Theatre Company at the Minneapolis Institute of Arts. In the same vein the trials experienced by the small circus group in *How Could You Tell?* dramatize the early struggles of Donahue and his fledgling theater company to establish themselves.

Like *Good Morning, Mister Tillie, Hang On to Your Head* is structured around a series of episodes and images culminating in a grand finale. As the play opens, children are being taken by their parents to a station where the children wait to embark on a journey to some unspecified destination. Whistles blow as the parents wave good-bye and leave the children at the station. Fog rolls across the stage and lumbering giants called Orgs sweep spotlight beams across the audience and the stage. All the children are carried away by the Orgs — all but Verleen, who escapes with the aid of magical, mysterious Uncle Harry and Leonardo, a companion Uncle Harry creates especially for her.

The three cavort in clown costumes, picnic together in the moonlight to the accompaniment of balalaikas, and perform magic tricks in a carnival; eventually Verleen and Leonardo become

Spanish dancers in a nightclub. Uncle Harry disappears. Meanwhile, Verleen's parents search frantically for their daughter; Mrs. Panky darts about, followed by diminutive, mute, cigar-smoking Mr. Panky. Verleen and Leonardo find the Garden of Eternal Peace, and there Leonardo also disappears. Verleen does not find Uncle Harry in the garden, but she discovers strength and the Holy Spirit within herself. Finally she emerges as the Queen of the World, triumphant and beatific, in a grand parade. Her parents, watching the parade, wave and marvel at the beautiful queen but do not recognize their own daughter.

In general, the story is about a young girl whose parents pay more attention to the mud she gets on her skirt while playing than to the beauty in her soul. Some parents have feared that in this play Donahue is encouraging the alienation of child from parent, which is quite the opposite of his intention. He merely reports that alienation does exist between some parents and their children, and he urges both children and parents to "hang on to their heads" and to proceed full tilt along the series of beautiful adventures that life offers: "I would like to suggest a modicum of madness for us all, the kind that causes speculation on the vocabulary of a marshmallow or how fast a group of us can run down the hall with kitchen pans strapped to our feet. The children know we have time for this before we go out and plant the garden and pave the streets, just as they pause to pray before they walk a fence. Children are reverently involved with the human dilemma, for their life is too sweet and the music too neat to take for granted."

The three plays in this volume were all produced by the Children's Theatre Company during the Easter season. Each emphasizes the theme of resurrection of the soul, and each in its own way pays tribute to the spiritual beauty of children. In each play some children are drawn more than others to the awareness of the Holy Spirit: Pat and Sara learn from Old Kieg and Mrs. Souss and acquire their magic; Emile and Jane are cradled by Elaine, and the three are observed and sheltered by the Old-Fashioned Man; Bubble and Black-Eyed Pea are drawn to each other and to the Matchbox House, which is filled with the Spirit. Donahue is especially interested in the unconscious spirituality of children: "Every day I see one or two children who do not hesitate to indicate a secret knowledge bursting at the middle. 'Teach me how to fly and I'll show you how to sail through walls! Show me how to talk like velvet and I'll drive the Boogie out of your cellar!' One must sense these things, of course . . . they never say straight out, never face to face, 'I wish to be an artist'; but they say it in a sly and silly way, while peeking out between the curtains in a hat or laughing like a witch in the bedroom or pretending to be a high priest over the piano bench on a rainy day with a towel and a sacrament of Necco wafers."

Old Kieg of Malfi, which followed *Hang On to Your Head,* was again organized episodically with no real plot. It is simply the story of two extraordinary people living in a cluttered old room on 1014 Street; they draw the neighborhood children into their magic and eventually bequeath their spirits to the children. The play marks a departure from Donahue's earlier plays in that it uses a realistic setting and it experiments with language as the earlier plays had not. Fantasy and realism constantly intermingle as the actors, in realistic situations, indulge in free association with words and actions. For instance, Johnny imagines how nice it would be to be as tiny as an ant, but he wants assurance that he would be able to wear clothes even if he were tiny.

In *How Could You Tell?* Donahue undertook a much more complex play. For the first time he developed his characters in the context of a plot that contained suspense, conflict, and a resolution, and he began to explore new ways of handling dialogue and multiple, overlapping speeches. The inspiration for the play, its title, and the character of the Old-Fashioned Man, came from a real-life scene that Donahue observed in a Minneapolis restaurant. A local ex-fireman (the "Fasty" to whom the play is dedicated) often performs a delightful improvised dance in and out of the tables in the restaurant. The dance is graceful and idiosyncratic, quite unlike any known "social" dance, at times gliding and at times a series of unpredictable stops and starts. Fasty's head constantly turns from side to side, following the darting movements of his eyes as he surveys the room. Once when he was dancing past a group of businessmen, one of them stopped him and snorted, "Just what in the hell do you think you're doing?" Fasty paused in mid-pirouette, winked, and replied, "How could YOU tell?" — and danced away. As the Old-Fashioned Man in the play dances and mystifies the circus folk, he transforms Fasty's self-assurance and freedom into a challenge to the dying circus.

Donahue's third play, *The Cookie Jar*, fully utilizes plot, characterization, and language. Written specifically for teenagers, it is explicit in its message ("find the life that's good and simple"), contemporary in its use of slang and caricature, and almost melodramatic in its plot. The audiences of teenagers and their families responded to Donahue's broadly sketched play and Roberta Carlson's hand-clapping, toe-tapping score, and *The Cookie Jar* did very well at the box-office.

The development of the plays in this anthology was supported by a three-year grant of $250,000 made to the Children's Theatre Company by the Rockefeller Foundation in 1971. The purpose of the generous funding was to enhance the concept of special theater for children by giving the company the opportunity to enlist poets, composers, and other artists in the writing and the production of children's plays. The Rockefeller Foundation also enabled the theater to create a department that could prepare scripts of the plays for publication and distribution. (Personnel in this department also made videotapes and tape recordings of the productions, helped to assemble photographic archives, and copied music for a number of new scores.)

Up to this point only fragments of the scripts for *Old Kieg of Malfi* and *How Could You Tell?* were available in written form, and the stage directions and the musical scores existed almost entirely in the minds of Donahue, the composer, and the staff members who had taken part in the productions. Eventually a crude tape recording of *Old Kieg of Malfi* turned up, and various scenes and speeches were reconstructed (in part from notes that Donahue had scribbled on napkins at suppertime script-writing sessions in a nearby restaurant). Finally the work was finished, and the complete scripts appear in print for the first time in this book. The preparation of the script and the score for *The Cookie Jar* was less haphazard, mostly because the

Rockefeller grant enabled the staff to tape the production and to formulate the stage directions while the show was being produced. (Excerpts from the score are footnoted in the script to indicate the pages on which the music appears.)

Since the blending of visual and musical elements is such an integral part of Donahue's plays, many people who have followed the work of the Children's Theatre Company over the years have expressed some astonishment on learning that the plays are being made available in book form. The scripts in this volume represent an attempt to translate the playmaking techniques Donahue uses in his works into a form which will enable other theater groups to share the plays with children in their own communities. Beyond this, however, it is hoped that the ideas, methods, and artistic goals inherent in these plays will help to encourage the development of innovative dramatic works for children, teenagers, and their families.

Linda Walsh Jenkins
Editor

The Cookie Jar. "It's kind of magic. I just push on the keys and out comes the music." (Photograph by Gary Sherman.)

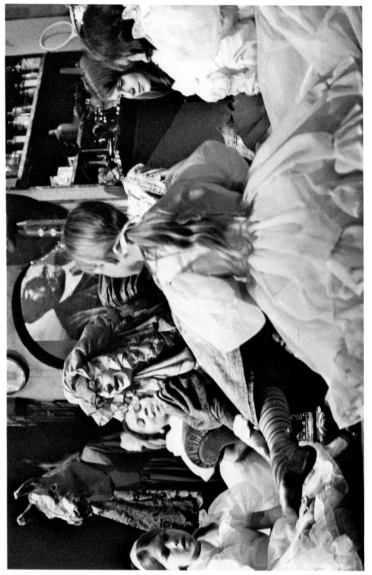

Old Kieg of Malfi. "These, girls, are dancing shoes . . . toe shoes."
(Photograph by C. T. Hartwell.)

Old Kieg of Malfi. "Yes, the bird plays the piano. Want to listen?"
(Photograph by C. T. Hartwell.)

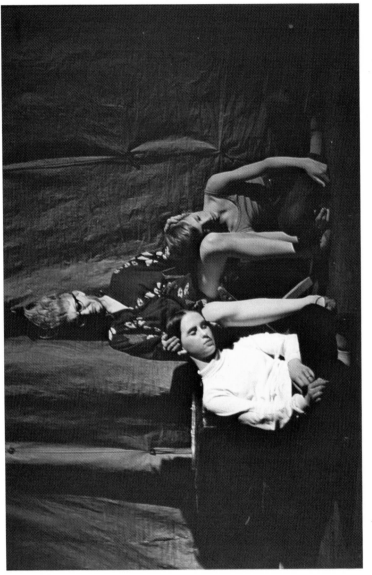

How Could You Tell? "Now go to bed . . . my little birds . . . my little flowers . . ."
(Photograph by the Children's Theatre Company.)

The Cookie Jar and Other Plays

Old Kieg of Malfi

CANDACE

*I would like to be quite ugly . . . have a face like an old toad pot . . .
with old fat hands and eight-foot knees like old lump face. Like
old stink pot toad . . . with old leather lace-up shoes . . . up to
my neck with a skate sock for a face . . . for a head. And then
walk into my mother's house and to my teacher's, into the
church, to the library, and say, "Hello! I'm ready to be married —
don't you like the way I look?"*

Dedicated to Martin Luther King, Jr.

Old Kieg of Malfi was first produced by the Children's Theatre Company of the Minneapolis Society of Fine Arts in March 1968. The script was edited by Linda Walsh Jenkins with the assistance of Carol K. Metz.

Cast of Characters

Old Kieg
Mrs. Souss
Karlis
Linda

Telephone man
Household moving men
Offstage voices of a
   man and a woman

Children: Sara, Pat,
Candace, Tim, Mike,
Richard, Barry,
Teddy, Kathy, Artie,
Dale, Peter, Gary,
Elaine, Joe, Bridget,
Johnny, Ginni

NOTE: Except for Old Kieg and Mrs. Souss, the given names of the actors were used.

Sequence of Scenes

Prologue	Gospel Singing
Scene i	"Lessons in Love Scenes Given — 1014 Street"
Scene ii	Children Playing; Sweet Air — Free!
Scene iii	"To Win the War — Meet Me. 1014 Street"
Scene iv	The Young Poets
Scene v	The Old-Fashioned Boot
Scene vi	The Ugly Starlet
Scene vii	Haikus
Scene viii	At Home with Old Kieg and Mrs. Souss
Scene ix	Magic and Science
Scene x	The Acting Lesson
Scene xi	How Old Kieg Ended the War
Scene xii	The Birthday Party
Scene xiii	The Transformation

Notes on the Play

Old Kieg and Mrs. Souss live in the cluttered attic of an old Victorian home at 1014 Street. The children of the neighborhood gather there to hear fanciful tales and to travel in spirit through past, future, and timeless visions. Old Kieg and Mrs. Souss are out-of-time, and their deeds are from the realm of wizards. The children rendezvous at 1014 Street in search of the eternal life of the spirit, and the attic becomes a special playground for them. There they imitate exotic Eastern dancing, laugh at a parody of teachers in Old Kieg's Kool-Aid speech, and create magic tricks. Finally Old Kieg transforms himself into pure spirit, Mrs. Souss mails herself away, and their spirit passes into a young boy.

A cutaway of the upper story of a house fills the center and the left side of the stage. Downstage of the house is the street in which the children play. A door at downstage left opens onto a concealed stairway that leads to the interior set; the primary playing area, the attic room in which Old Kieg and Mrs. Souss live, is screened behind a gray curtain until the scene "At Home with Old Kieg and Mrs. Souss." The principal features of the attic room are a stained glass window at upstage left, an old upright piano along the wall at the left, a coat rack with a horse's head on it against the right wall of the room, two overstuffed armchairs, and a table. The room is filled with odd items and mementoes such as a picture of Lenin, a big stew pot, a telephone that is not connected, shelves laden with bric-a-brac, and a conglomeration of keepsakes. At upstage center a curtained doorway

5

leads to an invisible extension of the attic and also provides access to a roof-balcony at upstage right.

The children are all dressed in contemporary clothing. Mrs. Souss wears a mobcap, a long dress of undefined shape and origin, and hiking boots. Old Kieg wears an odd wizard's hat (conical, with the tip flopping forward, not unlike one seen in a photograph of Salvador Dali), a plastic half-mask with huge pink cheeks, and a long robe that is open at the front over baggy trousers and a nondescript shirt.

Prologue   Gospel Singing

The cast, gathered onstage, sings "He's Got the Whole World in His Hands" as a film and slides are projected on a screen behind them. The theme of the images is brotherhood, compassion, the resurrection of faith, the flow of life through constant rebirth, and the betrayal of the Holy Spirit by man's inhumanity to his own brothers.

Scene i   "Lessons in Love Scenes Given — 1014 Street"

As the lights come up, Mrs. Souss is seen at upstage right holding a bowl of fish, and Old Kieg is downstage from her blowing soap bubbles from a bubble pipe. They are both dressed in yellow rubber raincoats. They pause, look around furtively, pick up their suitcases, and begin to exit at downstage left. They stop short as Candace runs in, followed by Tim, who grabs her hand and pulls her toward him. She resists, then they embrace and kiss. Mrs. Souss sings the love theme from Tchaikovsky's "Romeo and Juliet" and takes a snapshot of Candace and Tim, who run off, surprised. Old Kieg shines a flashlight on a sign at stage left that reads "1014 Street." Mrs. Souss ,

7

*removes from her camera a huge picture of a couple kissing, crosses
to center stage with Old Kieg following her, and tacks the picture and
another sign on the wall.*

MRS. SOUSS
   (*reading the sign*) "Lessons in Love Scenes Given — 1014 Street."
   (*Mrs. Souss and Old Kieg exit at stage left as Karlis leads Sara in
   past them. Sara stops when she sees the picture and the sign; she
   goes to the picture, studies it, takes it off the wall, and puts it in her
   coat. She walks back to Karlis, who grabs her hand and hurriedly
   pulls her offstage. Blackout.*)

Scene ii   Children Playing; Sweet Air — Free!

*Voices are heard in the darkness. Richard, Barry, and Teddy are at
one side of the downstage area. Sara, Kathy, Ginni, and Artie are at
the other side. The games and speeches in this scene contain freely
associated verbal imagery.*

KATHY
   Oh, don't touch me. I'm the electricity girl and you'll get killed.
SARA
   Down in the swamp.
A WOMAN
   (*calling from offstage*) Laurie, Laurie Ann, you get on home!
TEDDY
   Ash can, ash can, hit the bash can.
KATHY, SARA, GINNI, and ARTIE
   (*chanting as though jumping rope*) Grace, Grace, dressed in lace,
   went upstairs to . . . powder . . . her . . . face.

A MAN

(*calling from offstage*) Lincoln, you get on in here!

KATHY, SARA, GINNI, and ARTIE

Red Rover, Red Rover, send Poolieeee . . . (*The girls exit. When the lights come up, Richard, Barry, and Teddy are playing leapfrog. When the game is over, they flop down on the floor as Kathy, Sara, Ginni, and Artie enter skipping; they form a circle, dance under each other's arms, twirl, curtsy, and fall to their knees. Immediately Richard leaps to his feet and skips in a circle around the boys, patting each one on the head.*)

RICHARD

Orange duck, blue duck, aqua duck, red duck, gray duck . . . (*He runs around the boys and sits down in his starting position. The girls applaud him and stand up.*)

SARA

Who will draw the frying pan?

KATHY

(*making a huge circular motion with her finger in the air*) I will draw the frying pan.

SARA

(*pausing between words*) Who . . . will . . . put . . . the . . . bacon . . . in? (*The boys make a circle around Artie with their arms. Then all the boys and girls except Artie turn and face the audience in a line with their hands behind their backs. Artie weaves in and out among them and walks downstage to address the audience.*)

ARTIE

Everybody loves me because I'm so kind and sweet. (*She curtsies and runs to tag Teddy on the shoulder, then runs to the girls. Teddy snaps his fingers disgustedly because Artie got away, then puts his hands over his eyes. Richard and Barry walk in a circle around him.*)

BARRY

(*teasing Teddy*) Blind man, blind man!

RICHARD

Hee hee, can't see. (*Teddy reels to one side. A baby carriage whizzes toward Kathy from the wings; she trundles the carriage across the stage toward Teddy. As Kathy pulls Teddy's hands from his eyes, he drops to one knee and pleads for her hand in marriage.*)

TEDDY

Ah, Mrs. Alley Rolly Ball, will you marry me? I am the prince of cards and I am very rich. (*He rises and offers his arm to Kathy, but she doesn't take it.*) And I have pets at my house and lots of money. (*She refuses him again. Teddy suddenly drops to his knees, ignoring Kathy, and begins drawing in the dirt with his finger.*)

KATHY

(*to the audience*) My dress is quite rich, you know, of the expensive type, the kind a queen would wear. I had it especially made for me by many men who work for my dad. (*Sara sticks an imaginary gun in Kathy's back. Kathy turns, walks behind Sara, and puts a gun in Sara's back. Sara raises her hands and they walk away. Barry and Richard pretend they are driving a car; Barry is in the front seat driving and Richard is in the back seat. They stop the car and get out.*)

RICHARD

Bumpy ride, eh?

BARRY

Yes. (*tieing his shoe*) The president of the country isn't in right now, but I, being his righthand man, will take care of you. (*They walk upstage.*) Now over here we have . . . (*Artie and Teddy are rolling a ball back and forth.*)

ARTIE

I'm my mother.

TEDDY

Yes, I could see that, yes.

SARA

(*blowing soap bubbles*) I am one of the angels and I can fly as high as I want to and become invisible when I want and I don't have any feet and I can still walk anyway and I don't need wings. I don't have any wings. I have a jet dress. (*Kathy stands behind Sara and they walk backward, pretending to fly a jet plane. Barry, with Richard riding on his back, pretends to be a flying horse. Kathy pulls Barry by the hair.*)

RICHARD

I can build anything I want as high as anything or as big. (*Richard, Barry, and Kathy fall down. Kathy and Ginni begin playing "hopscotch."*)

TEDDY

Run faster than the fastest. (*Richard throws a stone to Kathy.*)

KATHY

My stone, please. You're welcome, you're nice, I love, love . . . (*Kathy and Ginni drop to their knees. Barry throws a rope to Richard and they turn the rope for Sara to jump.*)

ALL

(*chanting as Sara jumps rope*)
My mother, your mother
Live across the way.
Every night they have a fight
And this is what they say,
"Icka bicka soda cracker,
Icka bicka boo,
Icka bicka soda cracker,
I . . ."
(*They all drop to their knees except Sara, who walks in circles at center stage.*)

SARA

Thank you, thank you . . . (*She drops to her knees. The following lines are spoken in quick succession and almost overlap.*)

ALL

You're welcome, you're welcome.

BARRY

Goodnight, Grace . . .

SARA

Full of grace . . .

RICHARD

Will you marry me?

KATHY
    A frying pan?
TEDDY
    Who will draw . . .
ARTIE
    Your prayers.
BARRY
    I . . .
TEDDY
    . . . hate . . .
RICHARD
    . . . you! (*The children sing "Amen!" in choral harmony and
    stretch out on the floor and fall asleep. A glob of dough flies in
    from offstage left and falls in front of Sara. She picks it up, rises,
    and reads with interest from a flag on the dough.*)
SARA
    "Sweet Air — Free! 1014 Street. See Mrs. Souss." (*She puts the
    dough in her pocket. Blackout.*)

Scene iii   "To Win the War — Meet Me. 1014 Street"

*Dale, Peter, Gary, Joe, Mike, and Pat are playing cards as they
lounge together in a bull session, trying to impress one another.*

JOE
    Bull Tweedy, man!
PETER
    Oh, yeah?
MIKE
    Yeah!
PETER
    Hey, listen to this. There's these two guys in a bar, and one says to
    the other one . . .

MIKE

    Hey, what's your name?

DALE

    Tex.

JOE

    I know where you come from.

PAT

    Texas!

DALE

    Nope. I come from Louisiana.

PAT

    Then how come they call you Tex?

DALE

    Because I don't like to be called Louise! (*Pat snatches Dale's wallet.*) Hey, gimme my wallet!

MIKE

    Tough tinny, said the Winny.

DALE

    Yeah?

MIKE

    Yeah. Tough tinny, said the Winny. (*Mike throws Dale to the floor. The other boys gather in a group to look at the pictures in the wallet.*)

JOE

    Hey, look! Here's a picture. (*Mike takes the wallet and throws it to Dale.*)

DALE

    That's my brother.

GARY

    Aw, go on.

PAT

    Who's that? Your mother? Looks more like a man. (*Joe grabs the wallet.*)

JOE

    Pepper lies, Pepper lies.

PETER

Pepper thinks he's hot. (*The boys push Dale, pretending to fan him with their hands.*)

DALE

Yeah, he's in the army and I'm going too. For neat, man. Flying. Buzzin' out. (*Dale holds his arms out and pretends to fly. The boys shoot him down. Elaine crosses the stage doing a bump-and-grind in a silver lamé micro-mini dress, stepping over Dale's prostrate body. As she passes, the boys all whistle, aim darts at her, and make bomb noises. When she turns to look at them, they look away. Joe makes airplane noises. The boys all participate, pretending they are flying.*)

MIKE

Can't see the ground, just buzzin' out.

PETER

Now I see it.

GARY

I can see the trees . . .

PAT

I can see the fences . . .

MIKE

I can see the dogs . . .

PETER

. . . the horses . . .

GARY

. . . the people . . .

JOE

I can see their mouths . . .

PAT

I can see their lips . . .

MIKE

I can see their teeth . . .

ALL

Boom!!!!

JOE

You drop the bomb!!!!

ALL
Ahhhhh . . .

DALE
Nope, my hatch is stuck, and I fly off and never come back.

GARY
Chicken.

PAT
Shut up. (*Mike returns to playing cards; the others except Dale join him.*)

MIKE
Your deal. (*Dale sinks to his knees and crawls back to the others. Mrs. Souss rushes in, making a "putt-putt" noise like that of a dime store airplane. She throws her purse at the boys as though it were a bomb and runs offstage. Pat runs after her while the boys gape at the purse.*)

JOE
See if there's a name in it. (*They open the purse and take out a portable record player and a 45 rpm record. Pat rushes back in alone and joins the boys in the center of the stage. They put the record on the player and the voice of Mrs. Souss is heard.*)

MRS. SOUSS
(*speaking over an offstage microphone*) To win the war—Meet me. 1014 Street. (*A tape recording of a jet airplane is heard. The boys look up, trying to locate the airplane. Blackout.*)

Scene iv   The Young Poets

Gary is sitting in a pool of light on the edge of the apron, holding a
book. Old Kieg speaks from behind the gray curtain, inside his house.

OLD KIEG
> Did you get your homework done?

GARY
> No. But I would like to be done so I could rip my book up and eat
> it for a sandwich . . . that's what it's good for.

OLD KIEG
> Oooooooooh?

GARY
> Yup . . . Eat a book a day for a book sandwich vitamin . . . It
> prevents empty head cramps . . . in your butt.

OLD KIEG
> What?

GARY
> In your cigarette butt.

OLD KIEG
> Oh.

GARY
> In your butter butt . . . your boat . . . bill . . . book . . .
> ball . . . brown . . . bat . . . (*He giggles in between these*
> *bits of inspired alliterative prose. The lights fade down. Gary*
> *lights a large sparkler which flares brightly in the darkness.*
> *Another sparkler flares on another part of the stage where Tim is*
> *reading his work aloud.*)

16

TIM
>Evening is a little boy
>With dark wind-rushing hair
>Who skips the stars like stones
>Across the darkling pond of air.

GARY
>(*reading from his book*) Eighteen million Chinese coolies were punished for being too slow, so men took clubs and whips and beat them on their heads until they were all dead.

TIM
>Did you get your homework done yet?

GARY
>Yup. (*Blackout.*)

Scene v   The Old-Fashioned Boot

The pianist in the orchestra plays "Has Anybody Seen My Gal?" Mrs. Souss straddles a chair, her back to the audience. Bridget sings and tries to dance as Mrs. Souss beats time and shouts directions.

MRS. SOUSS
>Right and slide and left and slide and circle, circle, circle . . . Put your heart in it! (*to the pianist*) Esther! Esther! (*The pianist stops playing.*) Take it again from (*singing*) "covered with furs." (*The pianist resumes. Mrs. Souss and Bridget sing the phrase; Bridget continues to dance and soon her shoe flies off her foot. She turns to the pianist.*)

BRIDGET
>Esther! My shoe came off! (*Mrs. Souss hands Bridget a beautiful old-fashioned boot.*)

MRS. SOUSS
Here!

BRIDGET
(*dazedly taking the boot*) That's not my shoe.

MRS. SOUSS
Yes, it is. I have the other one at my house. 1014 Street. (*The pianist resumes with "has anybody seen," then stops, leaving a confused Bridget to sing a solo "my." Blackout.*)

Scene vi   The Ugly Starlet

A pool of light falls on Candace, who wears a lovely gown. She lights a cigarette and throws a kiss to the audience.

CANDACE
I would like to be quite ugly . . . have a face like an old toad pot . . . with old fat hands and eight-foot knees like old lump face. Like old stink pot toad . . . with old leather lace-up shoes . . . up to my neck with a skate sock for a face . . . for a head. And then walk into my mother's house and to my teacher's, into the church, to the library, and say, "Hello! I'm ready to be married—don't you like the way I look?" (*Mrs. Souss enters wearing an ugly mask; she hands Candace a mask like hers and then exits. Blackout.*)

Scene vii Haikus

FIRST HAIKU. *The action of each haiku is isolated by stage lights. Blackouts occur between haikus.*

LINDA
(*shaking Kathy's arm and lecturing her*) I'll teach you to play with matches, playing with matches, with matches, you and your matches, and your chemistry set, and matches, and matches, matches. (*Linda's voice stops but her mouth keeps moving. Kathy withdraws her arm, smiles and curtsies to Linda, curtsies to the audience, and turns back to Linda, still smiling. Linda resumes shaking her arm. Blackout.*)

SECOND HAIKU. *Teddy and Artie are walking on the edge of the stage as though walking a tightrope. Teddy leads.*

TEDDY
Now you let me go first on the tightrope because I'm the head tightrope walker. I'm the star and you're my assistant, so you walk behind with a pole to steady the rope—OK, Artie? (*Artie stops walking.*)
ARTIE
Yup. (*She pushes Teddy off the stage, then continues walking as the lights fade out. She imitates Teddy's speech and walk.*) Now, Artie, you let me go first on the tightrope because I'm the head . . .

THIRD HAIKU. *Joe, Pat, Dale, Gary, and Mike run down to the edge of the stage one by one, tossing imaginary stones in the direction of the audience.*

19

JOE
    Mine.
PAT
    Huh.
DALE
    Crap.
GARY
    Pretty good. (*As Mike throws another stone, everyone watches intently.*)
PAT
    Out of bounds.
ALL
    (*quietly*) Yeah. (*The boys form a semicircle with their backs to the audience. Blackout.*)

FOURTH HAIKU. *Richard and Johnny are sitting on the floor.*

JOHNNY
    Wouldn't it be nice, if we were real tiny? Then we could walk under doors, inside anything at all, like the little people do.
RICHARD
    How small do you mean?
JOHNNY
    Real tiny, the size of ants or something. We'd wear clothes, though, wouldn't we?
RICHARD
    Well, maybe. (*Blackout.*)

FIFTH HAIKU. *"Pomp and Circumstance" is heard as Sara enters slowly and walks to center stage. The music stops as she stops.*

SARA
    (*solemnly*) I won a yo-yo contest once. (*Loud applause and cheering are heard from offstage. The light remains on Sara. A low hum is heard; as it begins to rise in volume, a dim light comes up on the children at the center. They hurtle off the stage like*

*airplanes and run up the aisle to the back of the theater. The noise
reaches a peak when the children reach the back of the theater,
then fades out slowly. Sara's light fades to nothing with the
sound.)*

Scene viii   At Home with Old Kieg and Mrs. Souss

*Old Kieg is at the piano, playing and singing "The Old Piano Roll
Blues." A shaft of light through the upstage window gradually
illumines the details of the interior. As Old Kieg rises from the piano,
the pianist in the orchestra picks up the tune and continues playing it.
The sound of chiseling is heard; it seems to come from the attic. Old
Kieg walks to the window, looks down at the street, then walks
toward the doorway to the attic and stops to listen to the chiseling
sound. He turns toward the audience rather absentmindedly and
removes the rubber overshoes from his feet. He throws the overshoes
out the upstage window, mumbling something indistinguishable
about overshoes.*

OLD KIEG

(*calling down to someone in the street*) You're welcome. I'll see
you, Poolie. Any time. (*He takes a stew pot from a shelf and puts
it on a table in the center of the room, now and then mumbling in
an odd mixture of English and gibberish, occasionally bursting
into bits of "The Old Piano Roll Blues." He realizes he has
forgotten his tall hat, which he takes from inside the piano and
puts on his head. Ingredients for the stew are distributed all
over the room. He moves here and there to find them and add
them to the pot. He throws the ingredients in, alternately matter-
of-factly, mysteriously, or with a flourish. Occasionally he refers
to a recipe book. He reads Tarot cards to the horse's head on the*

coat rack. Suddenly Mrs. Souss bursts in from the left on roller skates, wearing an oversized horseshoe around her neck. She carries a trombone case and a large stuffed partridge. She puts on an old dust cap and an apron. Old Kieg takes the horse's head off the coat rack and puts it on his head. As Mrs. Souss skates past him, Old Kieg takes off the horse's head, puts it on the dressmaker's dummy, blows a whistle, and throws a football at Mrs. Souss.) Mrs. Souss, catch! (Mrs. Souss catches the football, walks it up her leg, and talks to it.)

MRS. SOUSS
Helloooo, Mr. Football, I'm so glad that you've come for dinner tonight, football. We enjoy eating you up for dinner. Hey, old leather face, pass! (*She throws the ball to Old Kieg, who puts it in the stew pot. Then she flops into a big armchair to remove her skates. Old Kieg salts the ball, then opens the rear window and looks out of it through a telescope.*)

OLD KIEG
Mrs. Souss, the moon wasn't out today, though many other things were. (*He sits down at the piano and sings, preparing the stew with one hand. While he blows up a balloon, Mrs. Souss discovers a telephone, which is not connected, in the stew pot. She begins to converse with "the store."*)

MRS. SOUSS
Helloooo, is this the store? Good. Say, the store, send it over to my house, 1014 Street. What size? Oh, a size, long . . . Oh, not too . . . Mmmhmmm, real pretty type. What? Gems. Oh, the bird? Oh, the bird is doing fine. Listen! It even plays the piano. Yes, the bird plays the piano. Want to listen? Listen now. (*She holds the telephone by Old Kieg while he plays the piano and says "Peep, peep, peep!"*) Isn't that good, Mr. Windowshade? And guess what else it does, too! Yes, no fooling. Would you like to hear that? Here, listen! (*She gives the telephone to Old Kieg, who says "Peep!" into the receiver in a low, coarse voice. He puts the telephone into the stew pot and dances two bars of tarantella with Mrs. Souss, who plays castanets. She grabs the dressmaker's dummy with the horse's head, dances with it, and collapses in the*

armchair as the castanets clack out of control. A doorbell rings.)
Helloooo . . . (*"The Children's Theme" is heard, played on flute and piano.*)

CHILDREN
(*singing at offstage left*) Hellooo . . . (*Artie enters and Mrs. Souss ushers her up the stairs into the attic. The following lines are spoken over a microphone by children offstage.*)

FIRST VOICE
I know . . . they're in there . . . I seen the lady open the door and go in.

SECOND VOICE
I'm watching too.

THIRD VOICE
Well, I'm going.

FIRST VOICE
Aw, come on over . . . let's go see anyway.

THIRD VOICE
Don't tell your ma, though.

FOURTH VOICE
Diamonds!

FIRST VOICE
Rubies!

SECOND VOICE
Pearls!

FOURTH VOICE
Every kind of jewel in the world! (*The chiseling sound begins again. There is a knock at the door.*)

OLD KIEG
There's someone at the door, Mrs. Souss. (*Mrs. Souss opens the door.*)

TELEPHONE MAN
(*entering*) Telephone man! I'm here to install your new phone.

MRS. SOUSS
We don't need it. (*She puts the end of the telephone cord to the man's chest and imitates a telephone operator.*) Hello, may I help you? (*The man hands a telephone book to Old Kieg, who shows it*

to Mrs. Souss. She shakes her head to indicate that she doesn't want the book.) Huh uh!

OLD KIEG

Oh, well now . . . that's quite a thing for . . . It would be quite a thing for . . . (*Old Kieg tears the telephone book in half, puts it in the stew pot, and offers the man a sip from a spoon. He puts the spoon in the man's mouth. The man chokes and reels out, falling down the stairs. Old Kieg and Mrs. Souss laugh as Old Kieg reenacts what just happened.*)

MRS. SOUSS

(*squealing*) Old Kieg-a-weega! (*Old Kieg stops to listen, and Mrs. Souss leans against the table. They remain motionless as "The Children's Theme" is played on flute and harp. Again children's voices are heard from offstage.*)

ALL

Helloooo . . .

FIRST VOICE

Come on.

SECOND VOICE

Red Rover, Red Rover, I'm coming right over.

THIRD VOICE.

I have a jet dress.

ALL

(*making a jet sound*) Whooosshhhhh!

FOURTH VOICE

As it is now, and ever shall be, world without end. Amen. There, I'm done, come on . . . (*Flute and harp are heard again.*)

OLD KIEG

Well, Mrs. Souss, how did you do today?

MRS. SOUSS

Well . . .

OLD KIEG

Well, I think I'll just sit right down here and have myself a nice cool refreshing candy cigarette. (*He flops down in his chair.*)

MRS. SOUSS

(*crossing over to light his cigarette*) We'll see, we'll see. (*She removes the stew pot from the table, puts a mop in it, and begins to mop the floor with the contents of the stew pot. The chiseling sound is heard. As Old Kieg reads from the Bible, the children enter the house and sit around him, listening. Artie comes down from the attic and climbs onto Old Kieg's lap.*)

OLD KIEG

Say, Mrs. Souss, listen to this one. I read it in my book the other day. (*He reads from the Bible.*) "The Lord saw that the wickedness of man was great in the earth and that every imagination of the thoughts of his heart was only evil continually. And the Lord was sorry he had made man on the earth and it grieved him to his heart. So the Lord said, I will blot out man whom I have created from the face of the ground, man and beast and creeping things . . ." (*He continues to read as Mrs. Souss and the children sing the gospel song "In the Garden." The end of his reading coincides with the end of the song.*)

MRS. SOUSS and CHILDREN

(*singing*)

> And He tells me I am His own,
> And the joy we share
> As we tarry there,
> None other . . . has ever . . . known.

OLD KIEG

". . . and the birds of the air, for I am sorry that I have made them. But Noah found favor in the eyes of the Lord." (*The lights fade down and out.*)

Scene ix   Magic and Science

A drum roll is heard and Oriental music begins as the lights come up. Girls are lighting candles in Old Kieg's house. Mrs. Souss sings an Oriental melody to which the children contribute an occasional "nyaa

nyaa na nas." An Eastern atmosphere pervades the scene. The girls put their handkerchiefs or their hair across their faces and writhe like belly dancers. Richard trades hats with Old Kieg, giving him a swami hat or turban and putting on Old Kieg's wizard hat. Mike sits in front of Old Kieg. Pat and Joe pick Artie up, show her to the audience, then seat her on Mike's head. They stretch her out, supporting her at her head and her feet.

OLD KIEG
> Ladies and gentlemen, I now present to you the greatest trick in the world . . . the famous trick of the sawing of a lady in half.

CHILDREN
> Ohhhhh!

OLD KIEG
> You ladies who have fear and trembling at this, look to the foreign gentleman who is standing on your right side and lean on his shoulder if you feel faint. And now I shall reveal to you the famous Saw of Blood! (*He pantomimes revealing a large saw.*)

CHILDREN
> Ohhhhhhh!

OLD KIEG
> You scoff, you laugh, you scorn, but I tell you that this saw has seen more blood than the hair of a pig's head. Now I shall lower the famous Saw of Blood, of the famous princess, Princess Ming Ming Woo, toward the abominable abdominal reaches of this charming and lovely young lady. But first, let us pause for the prayer of incantation.

MIKE
> (*whispering*) No! No, not the prayer! My head!

OLD KIEG
> Dispense with the prayer. (*Mrs. Souss starts to sing and Old Kieg gives her a withering look that makes her stop.*) And now, ladies and gentlemen, I begin the sawing of the wooden box of wood. (*A sawing noise is heard over an offstage microphone. Artie screams.*) There, it is done!! (*He rips a piece of paper in two. While the children applaud, Joe picks Artie up and swings her around. Then the children rapidly perform magic tricks.*)

JOE

I will now turn Princess Weenie Wee into a stone! (*He taps Artie on her head. She falls to the ground.*)

ARTIE

I'm a stone. (*The children cheer.*)

PAT

I shall now swallow the Fiery Sword of Satan! (*He pretends to do so.*)

OLD KIEG

Oh, I'm fainting.

GINNI

For my next trick I shall disappear! (*She covers her eyes.*)

TIM

Now, ladies and gents, a rabbit out of a hat. (*He pulls Richard up as though pulling a rabbit out of a hat. Dale and Peter kneel together and Sara puts her head up behind them.*)

SARA

And now I produce the world's only two-headed man and one-headed woman!

BRIDGET

I will now turn a woman into a horse. (*She puts the horse's head on Mrs. Souss, and the children make neighing sounds.*)

MIKE

And for the grand finale . . . a mouse into a rhinoceros . . . (*He brings forth Candace from behind a cloth. The children all squeal, clap, yell, and dance. Old Kieg rises and the children hush.*)

OLD KIEG

And now we will turn our attentions to more serious considerations of diet and ectological numbers. Now over here on my wall, I have many shelves . . . (*pointing and tapping at them with a stick*) . . . of types. And . . . uh . . . on the shelves we have flasks of your larger and smaller ones. (*He lapses into German and gibberish. He begins to make Kool-Aid, talking to the children about colors. Some words are intelligible.*) Ein pitcher . . . das ist full . . . und wasser . . . What does "wasser" mean?

CHILDREN
> Water! (*The lecture continues as Old Kieg adds a powder to the water with great ceremony. He stirs the mixture with a ruler.*)

OLD KIEG
> Kool-Aid!

CHILDREN
> Yay! (*They clap and cheer. The following actions take place simultaneously, underscored by music. Peter imitates Old Kieg, holding Artie in his lap. Mrs. Souss plays the piano and Bridget imitates an opera singer. Pat wanders onto the roof to daydream. Old Kieg looks through a telescope. Candace and Richard drop things off the roof. Sara talks to the dressmaker's dummy. Mike pretends to smoke a long cigar. Others play and pantomime. Gary walks to the center with a pencil and a note pad. Everyone moves in slow motion at this point, then the action freezes as Gary speaks. The orchestra plays "My Bonnie Lies over the Ocean."*)

GARY
> Who skips the stars like stones across the darkling pond of air . . .

JOE
> Are you asleep? Hey, we've got to go! (*Gary hides the poem in his pocket. Sara walks through the doorway to the attic and onto the roof while the other children say their good-nights and leave Mrs. Souss and Old Kieg alone.*)

OLD KIEG
> Good-night, Mrs. Souss. (*Sara plays with a balloon, jumps off the roof, and runs out.*)

WOMAN
> (*calling from offstage*) Laurie Ann, Laurie Ann, you come home nooowwww . . .

Scene x   The Acting Lesson

Sara slips into her raincoat offstage and returns immediately with the photograph from scene i. She walks to the door at stage left and rings the bell. Mike and Joe run onstage, pushing one another. Sara watches. The boys exchange pushes, taunting each other until Joe finally hits Mike; they fight, rolling on the stage. Sara rings the doorbell again. Mrs. Souss opens the door for her. The sound of a prizefight bell is heard. Sara enters the house. Old Kieg observes the fight from the roof, where he sits on a canvas chair.

OLD KIEG
Here now, boys, don't be fighting in my yard. You boys get out of my yard. (*The boys exit. Mrs. Souss and Sara walk into the room.*)

MRS. SOUSS
So you want some lessons in love scenes? I see you've brought my ad. (*She takes Sara's hat and coat, hanging them on the coat rack.*)

SARA
Yes, I do.

MRS. SOUSS
Well, love scenes are the hardest ones, you know. So you want to be an actress and act out parts on the stage?

SARA
Yes.

MRS. SOUSS
Well, you've come to the right place. You wait right here. I'll go get my actress kit. (*Her voice trails off as she disappears into the attic. The chiseling sound begins upstairs. Sara looks around the*

29

room as though for the first time and listens to the chiseling. She starts up the stairs but is interrupted by Mrs. Souss, who comes back with a big box of paraphernalia.)

SARA

What's that noise up there?

MRS. SOUSS

Oh, HE'S working up there . . . building a large stone thing . . . you know, just chiseling away on it all the time.

SARA

What is it?

MRS. SOUSS

Well, I don't really know . . . it's stone and big . . . oh, very big . . . of course I've only ever seen the feet of it . . . only the feet are done, but they're very big, about as big as this piano, I would say . . . It's not finished yet, just the feet . . . but he keeps working on it, dragging buckets of dust and stuff in and out of here . . . So you want to be an actress? Well, here's an actress hat. For the part of the pretty one, like the parts you would be playing. I once played those parts myself. I'll show you what I mean. (*She turns on a radio. Soap opera music is heard. Old Kieg speaks from the roof.*)

OLD KIEG

. . . box tops to this station. Lux Radio Theatre presents "Luna Bunda."

MRS. SOUSS

(*imitating a radio heroine*) No, no, please. Please don't kiss me or I think I'll faint. (*She turns off the radio and rambles on to Sara about acting, meanwhile changing hats and picking up props to suit her fancy.*) And then, well, all love scenes aren't serious, you know, like in the comedies or musicals when we'd sing and dance. Why, when I was in the chorus of "Tulip Time," we girls all came out dressed as flowers with petals around our necks and we sang (*singing*) "Oh Lordie, How I Love You." And then we had some meaty roles. I remember one of my favorite was a drama I played in once. (*seriously, in a thick Southern accent*) "Oh, Henry, our land is all gone, our house is burned down to the ground. We have no money, no food — nothing. But that don't matter none,

Henry, because I still love you, Henry." Now for roles like that we sometimes speak in many accents and tongues. This one has a Southern accent. Can you do a Southern accent?

SARA

I don't know.

MRS. SOUSS

(*speaking in a Southern accent*) Well, I'll teach you how to do . . . (*in her usual voice*) Well, I'll teach you how to do a Southern accent. Listen now . . . Oh, Henry . . . (*Sara repeats what Mrs. Souss says. The "Oh, Henry" speech is rehearsed with suggestions by Mrs. Souss. After they work through it, Sara says the whole speech as Old Kieg creeps down the steps; he crosses to her and responds to the last line of her speech.*)

OLD KIEG

And I still love you, Mary Anne Belle. (*Mrs. Souss and Old Kieg applaud a delighted Sara.*)

MRS. SOUSS

Oh, this is Old Kieg and he's the actor in the house and I'm the actress. We'll teach you all about love scenes, because we've played 'em all. (*They sing and dance to "Moonlight Bay" for two bars, then switch to "Tea for Two," which they use as the basis for clowning and improvisation. Their antics become increasingly frenzied until Old Kieg calls a halt and recovers his dignity.*)

OLD KIEG

All right, now that's enough of this silliness! Come on, Mrs. Souss, up on the balcony. (*She climbs onto the piano.*) Now this is a bush (*indicating the chair*). Psst, Mrs. Souss, the window. (*Mrs. Souss pantomimes looking out a window. She whispers a description of the balcony scene from "Romeo and Juliet" to Sara as Old Kieg speaks.*) But soft, what light through yonder window breaks. It is the East and Juliet is the sun. Arise, fair sun, and kill the envious moon, who is already sick and pale with grief, that thou her maid art far more fair than she. Oh, 'tis my lady, it is my love . . . Oh, that she knew she were, but soft, she speaks. 'Tis not to me she speaks, but to two of the fairest stars in all of the heaven.

MRS. SOUSS

Romeo, Romeo, wherefore art thou Romeo? Deny thy father and refuse thy name. And if thou wilt not, be but sworn my love, and I'll no longer be . . . Mrs. Souss! (*The three laugh and clap as Mrs. Souss ushers Sara up the attic stairs. Old Kieg mumbles ad-lib phrases such as "Well, we do some Arabian . . ."*) Now go out on the roof and practice . . . Henry . . . oh, Henry . . . (*Sara goes onto the roof. Old Kieg sits at the piano and plays the "Romeo and Juliet" love theme or a similar love theme. Mike walks by the house as Sara practices her speech on the roof. The love theme continues under their dialogue.*)

MIKE

(*calling to her*) Hi! What are ya doin'?

SARA

I'm practicing love scenes in acting class. I take them here.

MIKE

Yeah? Like what?

SARA

Romeo, Romeo, wherefore art thou Romeo? Deny thy father and refuse thy name. And if thou wilt not, be but sworn my love, and I'll no longer be . . . Mrs. Souss! (*She laughs.*)

MIKE

Mrs. Souss! Is that your name?

SARA

No, my name's Sara. But if I were in a play, my name would be Juliet, and your name would be Romeo, if you were in the play. But then, what's in a name? That which we call a rose by any other name would smell as sweet.

MIKE

I take thee at thy word. Call me but love, and I'll be new baptized. Henceforth I never will be Romeo . . . See ya. (*He waves to her and runs out.*)

SARA

See ya. (*She waves good-bye to him. The "Romeo and Juliet" music changes into a popular song such as "It's Only Words." Blackout.*)

Scene xi   How Old Kieg Ended the War

The boys are in Old Kieg's house. They gather around him as he tells a story of his exploits in "the war." He wears an old helmet, armor, and other strange bits of war costume.

OLD KIEG

Oh, we ripped their heads off and tore 'em up . . . They were coming down the mountainside.

RICHARD

Were they running or walking or what?

PAT

They were sneaking.

OLD KIEG

They had used camels and trained apes throwing bowling balls at us . . . and trained birds were flying overhead . . . dropping down . . . and the tanks were there. But we could beat 'em because we had special bombs . . . no one thought up but me . . . I spent some time inside my tent, working on it, when the shells and spears were flying through.

DALE

How come you didn't have to fight?

MIKE

Were you scared?

PAT

And did you have hot barrels of burning wax?

JOE

And poison darts?

GARY

And pygmies?

OLD KIEG
  And we had to watch out, too, because I wasn't the general, and
  sometimes they, if we didn't behave, made us stand out in the cold
  without our clothes on . . .

MIKE
  For how long?

OLD KIEG
  A hundred and twenty-four hours or days at a time. And then
  they'd let out sacks of trained mosquitoes near us . . . and
  donkeys would chase us with their teeth chomping. But we turned
  and clubbed their heads off.

BOYS
  Oh yeah?

TEDDY
  Yeah, donkeys ain't so bad.

OLD KIEG
  And then the enemy got worse and worse and they come with
  flying ants and swords and the ants spit bullets out . . . and the
  whole army was going to walk on top of our tents and chew us up
  and spit us out like old gum under the seat in a movie
  theater . . . but then all of a sudden I perfected my special
  bomb . . . the bomb of bombs . . .

MIKE
  What bomb?

OLD KIEG
  No one was going to defeat us, and I called all the men together.

JOHNNY
  And the generals too?

OLD KIEG
  And the generals and every soldier, and I passed them out and
  when everybody had them, we climbed to the top of the nearest
  hill (*climbing onto a chair, facing the audience*) and let 'em
  fly . . . Kiggy, gegiggy, bing . . . (*He passes out marshmallows to the boys.*) The Marshmallow Bomb! (*All the boys and
  Old Kieg run to the edge of the stage and throw their
  marshmallows into the audience. Then they sit down to enjoy*

eating marshmallows themselves.) Yes indeed, my boys . . .
even the trained apes and the donkeys liked them marshmallows.

PAT

Did the tanks eat 'em?

OLD KIEG

And the generals and the men with the swords and the axes and
the machine gun birds too. Oh . . . yesss . . . and that's how I
ended the war . . .

Scene xii   The Birthday Party

A pool of light reveals Linda scolding Kathy.

LINDA

No . . . you're not going to any party for anybody's birthday.
And I don't care if the dress was a present and I don't care whether
she's magic or not . . . and I'll tell you another thing
. . . you'd better wear a hat in church. (*Blackout. Linda and
Kathy exit. The lights come up on Mrs. Souss, making a phone
call from her house. The telephone is still unconnected.*)

MRS. SOUSS

Hello, girls . . . it's my birthday today, you know . . . and I'm
having a party for myself . . . (*laughing*) And I don't know
anyone anyway but myself, and Old Kieg, and he's upstairs busy
working on his statue of something . . . Don't bring any candles
because I'm too old for the cake I'm having and I'm sending you
all some party dresses which are out in the tree in your backyard,
so quick run and get 'em before anyone sees you . . . Now bring
all the . . . (*The sound of her voice dies down, but her mouth
continues to move. A little girl's voice, imitating Mrs. Souss's
telephone conversation, is heard over an offstage microphone.*)

Hello, Ann . . . my mother is having a birthday party for me and I want you to come . . . it's today . . . Louise . . . Pam . . . Karla . . . and Barbara Ann Heckridge . . . loona . . . bunda . . . (*The voice fades out. Pause. A knock is heard from someone at the top of the concealed stairway leading into the interior of the house.*) I'm coming . . . just a minute . . . Come on in. (*She opens the door and all the girls enter dressed in white party dresses, carrying gifts.*) Oh, Kathy, you look so pretty in your new party dress . . . Oh Artie, a ratchet, how did you know . . . Oh, thank you . . . Let me look at you . . . (*She ad-libs remarks as she greets the girls and accepts their gifts.*) Mrs. Souss baked a birthday cake. See, "Happy Birthday." You can eat the roses off later. Now, girls, sit down around Mrs. Souss. (*She sits in the chair and they sit on the floor around her.*) Well . . . hasn't anyone noticed something different about Mrs. Souss today? Hmmm?

ARTIE
Your hair!

MRS. SOUSS
No, not my hair, Artie. Same old hair. This is something new that you haven't seen before. Look again.

KATHY
You look real nice.

MRS. SOUSS
Well, thank you, Kathy, but look more carefully, something new.

GINNI
Well, it's not your dress, because that's the same old one.

MRS. SOUSS
No, but you're getting warm. Look lower . . . lower . . . (*She extends her feet to display pink toe shoes. The girls "oooh" appreciatively.*) These, girls, are dancing shoes . . . toe shoes . . . Since it's my birthday today, I thought I'd give all of you a little treat and tell you about the time that Mrs. Souss was a ballerina. Oh, of course you don't wear those every day. Oh no . . . why . . . why . . . you carry them with you in a little hatbox

with a handle when you ride in the car — then put them on when you get there.

GINNI

Well, how do you do it?

MRS. SOUSS

Oh, well, you just sit down and put your feet in them while you're doing it. But first with a little cotton down in the toe to make it soft, and oh, the toe of a . . . wooden toe for standing up on . . . a new toe shoe . . . oh, girls . . . Well, I'll tell you. I had this teacher and her name was Mrs. Garland Valleyover and she was beautiful. In her pictures.

KATHY

What do you mean?

MRS. SOUSS

Well, she had pictures of herself in the hallway by the stairs where you went up to the studio. Different poses and costumes from dances and ballets and things.

BRIDGET

Tell us the kinds of costumes, Mrs. Souss.

MRS. SOUSS

Did you ever see costumes . . . oh . . . a gypsy costume or Spanish or a queen or a bird princess? I remember my favorite one where she was a snow princess . . . just like a snow princess where she jumped high, dressed all in white, up on her toes with her leg out . . . and I'd go down there every Saturday morning and we'd stand at the bar and really work . . . point and point and up and plié and point . . . point and point and up and plié and point. (*Isolated by a pool of light, she demonstrates as she speaks.*) Oh, we'd work until we were just exhausted. And then came the time when you gave your recital. There you were, out on the stage, in your costume and you'd put your new toe shoes on and you were dancing, with all the other girls, not making any mistakes, believe me . . . not with everyone out there. (*Slowly the girls slip away and exit.*) Oh, and everyone was out there — your mother, your father, your aunts and uncles. And the orchestra was playing in the pit . . . Oh, the most beautiful music to dance to . . . Chopin . . . and then at the end you'd hear the applause coming up over the orchestra. And you got to take a "grand curtsy." (*The lights come up and Mrs. Souss realizes she is alone. She pulls a pair of galoshes over her slippers, picks up a paper sack, and starts toward the door leading outside; she pauses to yell up the stairs to the attic.*) Old Kieg! I'm taking out the garbage! (*The chiseling begins. The orchestra piano plays "The Old Piano Roll Blues." Mrs. Souss clumps down the concealed stairway. The lights slowly fade out.*)

Scene xiii   The Transformation

A revolving mirror ball is the only light onstage; it evokes in the audience the feeling of being in space looking at the universe. Mrs. Souss is sweeping the floor in the house. She listens for chiseling, but she hears nothing.

MRS. SOUSS

Old Kieg! Old Kieg! Aren't you working? Old Kieg! I thought we were going to practice our dancing contest . . . and the dart game . . . Well, I'm going ahead on that horse-naming project . . . you know, the one for a million dollars for the cereal company? . . . and you . . . Old Kieg! . . . (*She calls up the attic stairs and looks for him.*) Oh well . . . (*Mrs. Souss tromps up the stairs. She sees Old Kieg sitting on a little canvas chair on the roof.*) Old Kieg! (*She realizes he can no longer hear her. She slowly goes back downstairs and picks up the telephone.*) Hello . . . I want you to pick up a package . . . 1014 Street . . . No, it'll have to go by air . . . quite heavy . . . I'd say . . . Ohhh . . . ninety-seven pounds . . . oh, roller skates . . . ohhh . . . one hundred pounds, I'd say . . . hmmmhmmm . . . at five would be fine. (*As the scene pro-*

gresses, Old Kieg slowly removes his mask and costume. By the end of the scene he is transformed—golden, shining, and young. Mrs. Souss calls out the window to someone.) Karla! Here's a hundred-dollar bill. *(She throws money out the window.)* Go buy a thousand stamps and bring the girls back with you . . . I've gotta mail a big box away and I just can't lick all those stamps by myself . . . Tell 'em all to come . . . I'll make some candy or something . . . *(Mrs. Souss shuts the window and drags a large cardboard box to center stage. She opens the lid and climbs in with the aid of a chair. She stops to write a note, which she reads aloud as she writes.)* "Dear girls . . . had to go out on an errand for Old Kieg . . . am sending a bunch of old junk and stuff to some friends in the country . . . please wrap the box for me and put on the stamps that Karla brings. I'll address it later. If you don't see me . . . Love, Mrs. Souss." *(She gets into the box, pins the note to the side, and shuts the lid. Blackout. Old Kieg disappears. As the lights come up again, Pat stands at one side of the stage, reading his moving-away letter.)*

PAT

"Dear Old Kieg and Mrs. Souss . . . I got up early this morning . . . on purpose . . . to walk in the rain, like you said to. Those secret places were just right, and I sang the tune we learned. Thanks so much. I don't know if I can come back again, 'cause we might move. I'm bringing you some string to fix your windowshade. Good luck. Pat." *(He takes the note to the door of Old Kieg's house. A mover in overalls is removing the box from the house.)* Is anyone home?

MOVER

(shrugging) I don't know . . . The door was open. *(He exits with the box. Pat goes into the house, calling for Old Kieg and Mrs. Souss. They are nowhere to be found. Silence. Pat looks everywhere. Disturbed, he goes up to the workroom and onto the roof. He pantomimes throwing open a window facing the audience. When he opens his mouth to call down to the street, a flute is heard instead of his voice. Children's voices are heard singing "Where are you?" The orchestra begins to play "Jesu, Joy*

of Man's Desiring"; the popular song "The Times They Are A-Changing" could be sung from the orchestra pit as a counterpoint to the hymn. Pat finds Old Kieg's robe and mask; he puts them on, goes to the table, and starts to stir the Kool-Aid. As voices sing the hymn on "la," the volume of the music swells and the play ends in a triumphant crescendo.)

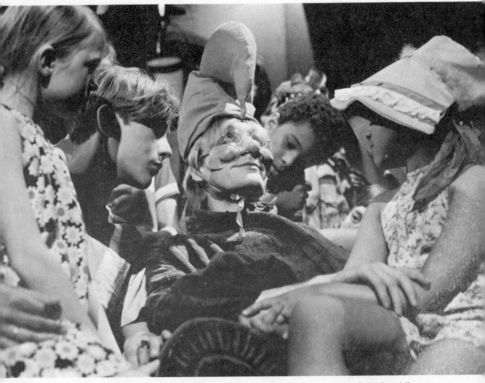

Old Kieg of Malfi. "But Noah found favor in the eyes of the Lord." (Photograph by C. T. Hartwell.)

How Could You Tell?

ELAINE
*I don't think about anything but the circus . . . that's what I
know, that's what I am, I guess . . . you little ones,
though . . . you got time to think . . . and time to fly.*

Dedicated to Fasty

How Could You Tell? was first produced by the Children's Theatre Company of the Minneapolis Society of Fine Arts in March 1969. The script was edited by Linda Walsh Jenkins with the assistance of Carol K. Metz.

Cast of Characters

Old-Fashioned Man
(the Holy Spirit)

Elaine Schmitt
(Onion Head Lady)

Marvin Carpentier
(Sword Swallower)

Pepper LeDoux (juggler)

Denise LeFleur (Poodle Lady)

Hélène Dufy (acrobat)

Martin Carson
(magician; circus manager)

Jane White (knife girl)

Barleen Toader (snake girl;
Picture Wonder Girl)

William Marble
(Tattooed Thin Man)

Lemo Guiderelli
(clown; owner of circus)

Emile Dufy (acrobat)

Eugene Hammer (barker)

Delores Oliveres (dancer;
showgirl)

Nestor Rope (knife thrower)

Gérard Dufy (acrobat)

Mike (boy clown)

Mario Guiderelli (boy clown)

Lars Tils (acrobat)

Giuseppi Guiderelli (boy clown)

Zoltan Capek (gypsy violinist)

Norma Teal (Fat Woman)

Irene Dress (fortune teller)

Maria Pamina (showgirl)

Nina Capek (wardrobe lady)

Eric Linds (acrobat;
Strong Man)

Grega Kaputkeck (juggler;
horse boy)

Nellie Jones (high wire acrobat;
showgirl)

Olga Deitz (horse girl)

Angela Martinelli (acrobat)

Camille Deitz (showgirl;
horse girl)

Gerhardt (singer)

Federico Pollo (roustabout)

Yves Doussette (acrobat)

Eve Chalk (showgirl)

China (midget clown)

Lucia Zuratt (midget)

Madame Prinskaya
(band leader)

Nettie Putz (juggler)

Claus Hentz (clown)

Sequence of Scenes

Notes on the Play

Lemo's small family circus is dying; attendance is very low, some of the young people want to leave to become farmers or perhaps just to fly away, accidents are frequent, and superstitions abound. The adults in the circus fight among themselves even as they remind the children of traditions and the old days.

When they put on their biggest show (a gaudy, tacky spectacular more suited to a supermarket opening than to anything remotely artistic), no one comes but a mysterious stranger who has been watching them. This stranger, the Old-Fashioned Man, tells them to toss out the old acts and the old show, to have faith in him, and to begin again on new soil. He assures them that their trunks won't sink, that they can set out to sea with their belongings and be assured of arriving safely on a new shore. He tells them, "I've been with you all . . . all of you . . . all the time . . . forever. The question is . . . are you with me?"

The circus people trust the Old-Fashioned Man. They take the circus apart, pack their trunks, and set out on the sea journey. They survive a storm and reach a new land that appears cold, deserted, and without water or shelter. When they open the trunks, they find water, seeds, plants, and hoes instead of the circus equipment. They begin to plant the seeds, working together and singing, young and old in harmony. They discover that one of the circus poles has sprouted leaves. The excited children begin balancing poles and rakes on the palms of their hands, juggling seed bags, and tumbling across the stage. A new circus is born of the old.

The basic unit for the setting is a large circular platform at center stage that is raked toward the audience; ramps lead offstage on both sides of it. The platform can be moved downstage so that it hangs slightly over the edge of the apron. There is a hole in the center for a pole. A curtain closes upstage of the proscenium from the right to the center, cutting across the center of the platform. There are also proscenium curtains. The back curtains and the platform are black. Most of the color of the play is provided by the circus costumes. Except for trunks and boxes, little stage furniture is needed.

Overture "In the Little Circus of My Mind"

A puppet theater with closed curtains stands in front of the proscenium. The Old-Fashioned Man enters, goes to the theater, and pantomimes dropping a coin in a slot. A ratchet sound is heard. The curtains of the theater open, and the Onion Head Lady's head and upper torso are seen. She wears a bib-costume that makes her look like a genie with crossed legs. She rests the legs of the costume on the sill of the theater and begins to sing. Her voice sounds like that of a talking doll, and she jerks her arms and head mechanically as she sings.

ONION HEAD LADY
>*In the little circus of my mind*
>*You can leave your cares and woes behind.*
>*You can fly around the moon,*
>*Take a trip in a balloon,*
>*In the little circus of my mind.*
>*(The Old-Fashioned Man looks at the audience. Blackout.)*

Prologue   The Amphora Brothers

The puppet theater, its curtains closed, remains onstage. There is a pole in the center of the platform, and against it leans a poster bearing the words "The Amphora Bros." The lights come up to spotlight the male acrobats, who stand in a human pyramid as the orchestra plays a fanfare accompaniment. The acrobats roll and somersault out of the pyramid and pose; they stand in a line with their arms thrown across their chests in a nineteenth-century circus strong man pose. Cheering and applause are heard throughout the act, and nineteenth-century American hats are thrown from the wings onto the stage.

Scene i   The Old Circus Trunk

Pepper watches as Marvin, the Sword Swallower, rummages through an old trunk. Denise, the Poodle Lady, speaks to Eve in French, telling her how to groom the dogs. Elaine and Jane are washing out dainties in a pail. Emile is exercising in the background. A flute player lounging nearby warms up. Sounds are heard from offstage: conversations, an engine starting up, snatches of circus music. Marvin finds an old photograph in the trunk.

MARVIN
    Look at this, here's a one . . .

48

PEPPER
  What?

MARVIN
  Ooh, wee wee! If that isn't a one . . .

ELAINE
  What?

MARVIN
  The old Ampora Brothers . . . And with their Dad . . . here
  too . . . His name was Dan Ampora.

ELAINE
  (*correcting him*) Amphora, Amphora — not -pora, -PHORA
  . . . (*Hélène enters, apparently on her way to a destination on
  the opposite side of the stage.*)

DENISE
  (*stopping Hélène*) Quand tu reviens, apporte-moi quelque
  boisson.

HELENE
  De quelle sorte?

DENISE
  Grape. (*Hélène nods and exits.*)

MARVIN
  It was an act of acts. Look at the faces, are these faces? Are these
  faces?

PEPPER
  Yes.

MARVIN
  Huh?

PEPPER
  Yes, sir. (*Martin enters and is stopped by Denise. He pauses by
  her, trying to disengage himself from the conversation.*)

DENISE
  N'oublie pas ce que tu m'as promis hier soir?

MARTIN
  Yeah, yeah.

MARVIN
  Martin, say, Martin—are these the—uh—come 'ere—Is this you?

Here, behind that thing! (*Together they scrutinize the old photograph.*)

MARTIN

Let me see—no . . . but it could be. What is this? Oh, now THERE is a circus. Do you know they had more feet of tent than any other outfit ever and way back then, too! What days . . . What's this? (*He points to something in the photo and they laugh.*)

MARVIN

No wonder people stood out in the rain to see this. Look here . . . this old letter. "Dear Mr. Sidds: We are going just great in the new act now. We do acrobatic specialty, with the high wire and slack wire and with the horses . . . We all juggle and Jack does the fire eat . . ." This part's torn off . . . something, whatever it was . . . "and over two hundred thousand people saw our act so far."

MARTIN

Say, can I have this? (*As Marvin nods his assent, Martin takes the letter and tries to leave, but Denise stops him.*)

DENISE

Ami, n'oublie pas, hein?

MARTIN

Yeah, yeah. OK. Sure. (*He leaves.*)

MARVIN

Anyway, that's what this trunk is full of, my friends, my dears, the tops . . . Emile, Jane, Miss Chalk . . . (*calling them over to him*) the tops of before you were born and I was a little rat of a boy . . . that's when the circus was the circus—in those days.

JANE

Why was it so good then?

ELAINE and MARVIN

(*almost simultaneously*) 'Cause it was . . .

ELAINE

No, 'cause it WAS . . . was BEFORE, when nobody can remember except dead people—ghosts. If you ask me, things are always the same, so you kids (*to the girls*) run down and get me some, ah . . . coat hangers. (*The girls exit. Hélène enters with a bottle of pop for Denise.*) Enchantée, madame, enchantée — hee hee (*teasing Hélène and Denise*).

DENISE

(*mumbling and laughing with Hélène*) Tête d'oignon . . . Horreur!

MARVIN

I'll tell you . . . I'll tell you . . . and you come here too—all of you. (*As Marvin talks, he arranges the people in a pose for a photograph.*) In those days people worked and people cared, for what you could do—with your hands, with your heart, and if it was beautiful, or great, if you could jump over the big cats, or do the triple, if you made a show go . . . with hard work and your own hand . . . two hands . . . then they loved you, and the circus folk worked—oh wee—they flew! And people loved it . . . appreciated it . . . yep, by the thousands of hundreds . . . umhuh. Folks worked hard for a cause and that cause was pride . . . and they never stopped until it was the very best you could do . . . on the horses . . . on the wire . . .

PEPPER

And juggling . . .

MARVIN

That's right—oh my children, oh wee, and then they even worked harder, laughin' and cryin' at the same time—'cause they was both in the blood forever . . . People came to come and see us . . . them . . . us, yeah — see us jump over the moon . . . and do you know why? 'Cause they, the people on the out-side . . . they can just sit out in the yard behind their old house and look at the big thing . . . But we could swing out and flip right over that moon and we still can. But now the people don't . . . think goin' over the moon's so much, I guess . . . these days. (*He becomes teary-eyed. To hide his emotion he looks into the viewfinder of a camera and takes their picture. The sound of a motor starting offstage is heard again. Everyone leaves to get ready for the performance except Marvin, Pepper, and Elaine. As Marvin begins to leave, Elaine stops him and hands him a coat hanger.*)

ELAINE

It is for you. Like to see you jump over this wire coat hanger before you try the Lord God's big moon. (*Marvin brushes past her and leaves, ignoring the coat hanger.*) Well . . . come 'ere. (*She and Pepper begin to hang costumes on hangers. Circus people prepare for showtime, busily crisscrossing the stage, talking, and rehearsing their acts. Acrobats tumble and practice flips; the wardrobe woman hurriedly pushes a clothes rack across the stage; Zoltan, her husband, follows her, playing the violin. Federico moves crates. Blackout. A spotlight isolates Barleen, who repeats her timeworn speech as if in a trance, her eyes glazed with boredom.*)

BARLEEN

My name is Barleen Toader. I am the original Picture Wonder Girl. Every inch of my body is decorated with artistic wonders from around the world. I am sixteen years old. (*The lights fade as she speaks.*) I come from normal parents. I have six brothers and four sisters. Come inside. For only twenty-five cents . . .

Scene ii   The Walk-Around

Lights and music gaily support the circus walk-around in which the performers parade before the audience. Eugene introduces the performers over an offstage microphone, often ad-libbing in foreign languages and gibberish. First the Big Heads reel across the stage; they wear enormous heads (Cat, Farmer, Pig Chef, and Freak) and appropriate costumes. Clowns bound onstage with their equipment: the facade of a house, a trick ladder, and buckets containing water and confetti. They quickly set up the equipment and begin their "elopement" scene while the other circus performers continue the walk-around. Jugglers dance and perform while showgirls and acrobats parade around the center platform in swirling capes and feathered headdresses. During the walk-around two clowns perform a bucket routine in which one throws a bucket of water on the other, then the wet clown picks up another bucket and throws its contents (confetti) at the audience. The elopement of a "girl" clown with a "boy" clown is capped by the arrival of "her" father and policemen. Sirens scream and spotlights sweep the stage. Blackout. The curtain upstage of the proscenium closes and the freaks line up in front of the curtain. The lights come up slowly on the freaks, who stand slumped and solemn as Eugene announces them over the microphone in gibberish and an ad-lib spiel about "the greatest freaks in the world." Sounds of engines starting, laughter, and whistles are heard from offstage. Blackout. During the blackout the curtain is opened.

Scene iii Signs and the People

The circus people are in the cook tent in robes and casual clothes. Some finish supper at the dining table while others play cards on a trunk. Their nerves are on edge. Sounds of thunder and rain are heard occasionally. Denise paces back and forth. Finally she throws down a tin plate and challenges Lemo.

DENISE
> Qu'est-ce que vous entendez, hein, hein? Je pourrais crever de faim! Et mes petits aussi, hein! Mes jolis, mes pauvres petits jolis! Et Hélène, là, et ses fils, abandonnés! Alors, si loin a ne rien trouvé que ceci, toujours! No people!

LEMO
> It will be better any day soon.

DENISE

Any day, any day, any, any! Je pourrais attendre trop (*indicating William*), jusqu'à devenir une momie, moi! (*Hélène laughs.*) Je quitte la boîte!

WILLIAM

What's she saying?

HELENE

She say you can turn into a mummy.

WILLIAM

Now what's she want to say that for?

LEMO

No, she says she is quitting. The crowds are too small. There is a small crowd . . . there is not enough money, not enough food. Not enough handclapping for her little doggies. (*More thunder and percussion sounds are heard.*)

DENISE

C'est une mauvaise signe, cette pluie!

HELENE

Oui, oui, et il fait froid aussi.

WILLIAM

What's she saying now, Emile?

EMILE

She say it is a bad thing, the rain.

WILLIAM

She ought to go out and stand in it. Might wash some brains into her doggie head.

MARVIN

Eat one of your dogs if you're so hungry.

DENISE

Eat a pack of swords and choke! (*to Emile and Gérard*) Ce fameux mangeur s'étrangle sur un bonbon! (*The boys laugh.*)

MIKE

What did she say?

HELENE

Hush. (*Denise stalks back toward Lemo, bumps into Camille, and scuffles with her until Lemo intervenes.*)

LEMO

(*rising*) These women are fools. And in front of the children. Fighting. Look. We all know business is bad, but so what? Sometimes business is bad, huh? So what are you going to do? Fold up? Sit in a puddle and cry? Huh? (*haltingly*) You should see . . . three years ago . . . when the snow was . . . The tent, it crumpled in under the weight of the snow. Push, push, so put it up again, the people come again. Huh, Gene? Huh?

EUGENE

Sure. Who worries? Last night was a good house, not as many as we would have liked for, but enough. The people are coming, they are just slow starting, don't worry.

ELAINE

Look! People is coming until their legs fall off and then they're coming again as soon as they find a way to get here.

MARVIN

You people are so stupid, I tell you. The circus is the circus, it always was and that's that. Now get backyard and get to working! It's showtime straight off. Go on and work your kinks, Hélène, Emile, Gérard. Go on, all of you. Work your kinks, work your kinks.

HELENE

OK! OK! When the crowd is not coming, we work harder, eh? then harder. We do beautiful and the people have to cry and laugh and cheer us, even though there is not many. They love us and tell their friends, then THEY come and everything is full in the tent again. (*She turns to her two sons.*) Uh? come on. Allez, allez! (*Others ad-lib: "Let's go!" "That's right!" Thunder is heard again. The lights go out. Instantly candles are lit. Delores hesitatingly delivers a speech to the audience in a single spotlight; it is a parenthetical moment, almost a flashback.*)

DELORES

But the other time, last night, in the show, the sideshow, I am feeling good and I look down and I see some face, dis face, those faces, a few faces, and I don't think they like me, my dance, and I am afraid that nobody likes my dance now. It is too old, perhaps.

The children, they have seen it and they don't want to see it, and I think perhaps I quit. There are so few people . . . and they don't smile too much. (*The lights come up again on the others; they ad-lib: "What's wrong?"*)

ELAINE
(*to Delores*) It's your costume, honey, let me talk to you about that part of your . . .

LEMO
(*interrupting*) Look. We, the circus, we make it through the fires—back up; the blow-down—back up; the water—back up. And always back come the people to see the circus. What makes you think it's any different? No. Let's get to work, eh? Come on.

NESTOR
What about the signs? Jane and me don't like them.

HELENE
Mais ces mauvais signes! (*The group ad-libs: "Bad signs!" "The signs!" They all talk at once, voicing fears and superstitions. Elaine stands on a chair facing the audience. She commands the attention of everyone in the cook tent.*)

ELAINE
Signs! I'll tell you about signs and people. Signs and THE people. One time we all knew things were in a bad way, like now . . . like they are now . . . rain, no crowds, and sure enough, that night during the animal act the tigers broke out and headed right into the audience. And what do you think? And what do you think happened, Michael? We all of us rushed out, scared till we were ready to melt on the floor, and we led that group of folk in singing hymns till those cats were got up and put back to bed. And them folks had God in the head. Now, how's that for a story of the circus and the people? That's what we ought to have around here — more songs to trade for these . . . long dog faces. (*She teases and mocks Denise.*) "Enchantey," madame . . . "enchantey." Did you see a sign? Well, here it is. Things don't change and people is people, and they're starting to come if I can hear at all. Now, Hélène, get to work! (*Elaine begins singing "Oh, Mein Papa," and others join her until they are stopped short by Emile, who has run to look into the wings.*)

EMILE
> Look, look, there's a lot of them, Mama! Tonight, we . . . we fly!

LEMO
> Tonight, we fly! (*Blackout. When the lights come up again, the center curtain is pulled three-quarters of the way across the stage. Federico stands at its onstage edge, taking tickets from a line of people; the people go behind the curtain after giving him their tickets. At the end of the line is the Old-Fashioned Man; he carries a potted plant, which he hands to Federico. The Old-Fashioned Man peers over his shoulder at the audience and shakes a foot slightly behind him as Federico regards the plant with surprise. Blackout.*)

Scene iv   "What do you want to be?"

Hélène, Emile, and Gérard are exercising in the back lot. Hélène and Gérard count in French as Emile counts in English, "one, two, three, four," over and over with them. Emile does not have his heart in the work.

GERARD
> (*to Hélène*) Emile est un idiot. (*to Emile*) You little nut head. (*to Hélène*) Maman, il ne travail pas. (*to Emile*) You are slow.

EMILE
> Uhhh! (*He makes a demeaning gesture to Gérard. Hélène admonishes them.*) It is you who are slow . . . in the head! (*The boys begin to fight. Hélène separates them and gestures for Gérard to go upstage as she seats Emile on a box.*)

HELENE
> Emile, mon cher, sit down. I know it is difficult for you to do the act, but Emile — ah, moment. (*She opens her purse and takes out*

a billfold with pictures in it.) Look! (*She laughs.*) Is this you? It could be, ah, Gérard? (*She holds up a picture for Gérard to see.*)

GERARD

Papa!

HELENE

There is a man . . . your papa. Oh, Emile, your father was one of the greatest of them all. Perhaps the best. And see how much you look like him. You were only three when he died and you never knew him. But he loved you so much, ah, oui, almost as much as he loved the circus. His life was the circus and so is yours, Emile. The circus . . . le cirque . . . Your papa, if he were alive, would tell you today, as he told Gérard . . .

EMILE

(*interrupting*) But Mama, I don't want to be in the circus!

HELENE

Then your papa would tell you today: Once you put on the tape and step into the ring you cannot turn back. Cannot change. No stopping. You are circus and circus is you. But still that is not enough. (*She pulls Emile up, stands him on the box, and slaps him into good posture as she speaks.*) You must do more. Why? To be a strong . . . a strong . . . pole . . . that pushes up the tent and holds it up. (*Other boys of the circus enter, drawn by the sounds of the quarrel.*) Braces it against all things—rain, wind, all that bad stuff—hold it up forever until you die. Not some weak little skinny rope of a boy that lets that big top fall. Do you hear me? Huh? No no . . . not me . . . do you hear the voice of your papa? Huh? (*She shakes him.*)

EMILE

Yes, Mama.

HELENE

Hey, people, right, right, huh? (*Other acrobats enter as she calls and gestures to them. Everyone claps and agrees with her.*) Good. Now, let's get to work. (*Others onstage cheer as the group does one stunt. Hélène balances on the feet of one of the men and is lifted into the air. Emile is supposed to be "spotting" for her, ready to catch her if she falls, but he is not paying attention. She screams, falls, and hurts herself.*)

GERARD

Emile, that was your catch! (*Hélène slaps Emile in the face and runs out crying. The other acrobats except Emile and Gérard follow her. Gérard and the boys tease Emile cruelly.*) Emile is going downtown tomorrow. He is going shopping. He is going to buy a new hat, and new shoes, and a tie, and a little suit, aren't you, Emile? Emile doesn't like the circus. Emile is going away from the circus, to be a big banker. (*During this speech the boys force Emile back onto the box and surround him.*)

MIKE

Or maybe to be a policeman, eh, Emile?

PEPPER

Or a nursey in a hospital, ha, ha.

MARIO

Emile should get a job in a rubber glove factory. He could use 'em.

GERARD

Well, what do you want to be? Huh? Huh? What do you want to be? Huh?

MIKE and MARIO

(*poking and shoving Emile*) Come on, tell us, huh, Emile? What do you want to be, huh, Emile?

GERARD

What do you want to be? TELL ME! WHAT DO YOU WANT TO BE? (*He shakes Emile and there is a long pause as the boys stare at Emile.*)

EMILE

(*softly*) A farmer. (*silence*)

MIKE

A farmer? (*All the boys break into raucous laughter, rolling on the floor in their glee. Emile attacks Gérard and a general melee begins. Elaine enters, sees it, runs off, and then returns with Lemo, Eugene, and Marvin, who break up the fight and send everyone out.*)

MARVIN

Here, what's this? You're so stupid, and right before the show, too. Get out of here and work your kinks, work your kinks! (*Emile is left alone. The Old-Fashioned Man appears and approaches him.*)

OLD-FASHIONED MAN

Pardon me, which way to it, son?

EMILE

The circus? (*He points in the direction of the show tent.*) The circus?

OLD-FASHIONED MAN

No.

EMILE

(*puzzled*) I don't know what you mean. I don't know what you mean. (*The sound of Eugene's voice announcing an act is heard in the distance; the circus audience responds with whistles and cheers.*)

GERARD and LARS

(*running onstage to Emile*) Come on, Emile, the show has started! We're on, hurry! (*The boys run out. The lights fade on the Old-Fashioned Man, who sits at center stage; he smiles at the audience and pantomimes fishing.*)

Scene v   High Wire Fall

An audience (composed of circus people in street clothes) is grouped around the center ramp, looking up as if watching a high wire act. Gerhardt, wearing a white tuxedo, stands on the ramp and sings a song in German to a waltz tempo. A turning mirror ball throws sparkling light throughout the theater. Eugene ad-libs an introduc-

tion to a special high wire stunt, the triple. A drum roll is heard. Suddenly there is a shriek from the crowd, then pandemonium ensues as everyone rushes to center stage. The lights black out briefly, then come up again. Nellie is lying in the center of the stage and Maria is crying over her. Sirens are heard. As Nellie is carried off on a stretcher, the clowns frantically try to divert the stage audience, blowing whistles as they perform the "elopement" sequence. A chaotic Mack Sennett scene erupts onstage and then ends abruptly in a blackout.

Scene vi   Something Is Up

All the circus folk gather in the cook tent; they ad-lib "I'm not standing for it!" "I quit!" and comments about Nellie's accident and other circus problems.

WILLIAM
   I tell you something is up, and don't try and say it ain't.
MARVIN
   I say it's . . .
WILLIAM
   You say nothing! You can pretend all you want, but look at it, no people but a handful to speak of, rain all the time so it's up to your neck in the mud and ain't that pretty. I guess not! And now Nellie falling from up there tonight! Well I'm spooked, I am. I don't mind saying it and I got me own ideas about it, too, I have . . .
LEMO
   What do you mean by that, William?

WILLIAM

There's something going on around here. I see. I see. I got eyes. Nellie falling's not the only thing. There's others! Didn't one of them little dogs of hers (*referring to Denise*) kick off? Colin breakin' his arm. Hélène laid up. Bad feelin's and all. I think somebody's trying something and I don't trust certain ones.

MARVIN

I know, I know. And the popcorn machine's broke. Big deal. Go count your tattoos, you old fool. (*William threatens to hit Marvin.*) Look here, you! (*Marvin and William begin to fight.*)

LEMO

(*breaking up the fight*) Wait, wait! There is something to what William says. Things are bad and I don't like it, none, either, but a little bad luck, it will go away.

MARVIN

I'll tell you how I see it. Certain things ain't up . . . That's the whole thing . . . ain't up . . . you know what I mean by it? That ain't work. That ain't circus. (*He looks around suspiciously.*) Now we ought to just sit down here now and list up certain people which ain't up. Certain acts which ain't up. And then just toss 'em out that flap. That's how I see it. Well, Eugene, whatta you want? You want to pay out good money for nothing? Bad luck, Lemo? No no. Just take a look at certain people what's in your circus.

HELENE

All right. Come out and say it. You think we not hold our own, eh? I know it's true. Well, what do you know? You . . . freak!

LEMO

Hélène!

EUGENE

What about that boy of yours, Hélène, that Emile?

NESTOR

Shut up!

EUGENE

You shut up!

MARVIN

Ohhhhhh . . .

EUGENE
Act! Why you're so tired, you're downright crummy.

MARVIN
I like your act all right (*chuckling*), the famous act of Eugene
shootin' off his mouth. Bang, bang! There go your lips! Bang,
bang!

LEMO
It will be better. Sssshhh . . . it will be better.

EUGENE
Shut up! Don't say that to me or I'll tell you how funny you are.
That ain't much these days. (*As Eugene attacks Lemo, a melee
erupts onstage. Blackout. A spotlight suddenly illumines a tall
clown on stilts and a midget clown, who fight each other with
huge boxing gloves in the center aisle of the auditorium. The
entire cast remains onstage in the darkness, laughing at them. The
Old-Fashioned Man is spotlighted in an aisle seat, holding a
helium balloon; the cast's laughter quiets. As the two clowns run
up the aisle to the rear of the theater, the Old-Fashioned Man
laughs uproariously. The spotlight lingers on him, then the lights
black out.*)

Scene vii   Knife Throwing

*Nestor and Jane practice their knife throwing act. Each time Nestor
throws a knife, the movement is punctuated by a rim shot on a drum.
Jane, who appears to be strapped on a wheel upstage, is unconcerned
about the knives. Nestor must mask the fact that the knives in his
hand are never actually thrown; a mechanism operated by a hidden
stagehand flips the knives into place from behind the board.*

NESTOR

And I'll tell you (*knife throw*), if that . . . (*He prepares to throw a knife but notices that Jane has stepped off the board and is inspecting something on the ground.*) What are you doing?

JANE

I thought I saw a dime.

NESTOR

Get back up there. (*Jane climbs back on the knife board.*)

JANE

Wasn't a dime, though. (*She nonchalantly scratches one of her legs.*)

NESTOR

If that Lemo (*knife throw*) . . .

JANE

Don't know what it was. (*She shrugs.*)

NESTOR

Doesn't (*knife throw*) get (*knife throw*) some people in here (*knife throw*) soon (*knife throw*) and stop (*knife throw*) saying (*knife throw*) any day (*knife throw*), I'm going to put one of these (*knife throw*) right through him. (*Blackout.*)

Scene viii   Lemo's Dream

A musical instrument simulates the buzzing flight of a fly, and the drum's punctuation of the knife throwing is suspended momentarily as a spotlight isolates Lemo and Giuseppi downstage center. The cast has assembled upstage during the blackout; they sit with their backs to the audience and they are not visible until they turn to face Lemo. Lemo wears a clown costume that conceals an enormous balloon on his stomach. He is following the flight of the fly with his hand, in

*which he conceals a straight pin. After a moment he pretends to see
the fly alight on his stomach, and he pops the balloon with the pin.
The same punctuation that accompanied the knife throwing occurs
with the popping of the balloon. The entire cast assembles in a semi-
circle in the darkness upstage with their backs toward Lemo and
Giuseppi. When the balloon breaks, Lemo and Giuseppi laugh
uproariously.*

LEMO

Ha ha, you like that, Giuseppi?

GIUSEPPI

Yeah, Papa.

LEMO

Pretty funny, huh?

GIUSEPPI

Yes, Papa.

LEMO

Good. Maybe I'll use that in my act. (*The lights come up on the
members of the cast as they turn to face Lemo.*) All right, all right,
we will do it — if the people do not come, we will MAKE them
come. Never mind the waiting . . . If they do not know we are
the greatest show, we will TELL them what they are missing!!!!
We will make them love us! We will drive them crazy . . . ha
ha . . . to see us. You want to know how I know this? Last night
I had a dream in my mind. And in it I saw a little circus, my circus.
(*The lights dim onstage; a spotlight isolates Lemo.*) OUR circus,
with all the people and the animals and the tents, everything. And
we travel around, all around, you know, looking for the people,
but we don't see. So finally, just as it is time to go to sleep that
night, I see some people out in a field, a long way away. And I cry
out, "Hello, hello!" And they answer back. (*He imitates voices
coming from far away.*) "Hello, hello!" And we are so happy. (*The
circus people around Lemo laugh and respond appropriately to
his story.*) And we all pack up. Roll 'em! Roll 'em! We go there
over the roads and hills through the mountains to the people, until
we are there, and what do you think when we get there? The peo-

ple are there too, but now they are huge — like giants — as big as trees in a forest — and their eyes and ears are so high up. They do not see us, so we start to unpack and set up. The motors are starting and they don't hear us. The tents are going up and they do not see, and I give the signal for the band to start playing. They play the biggest march we got, and the horses are running, the clowns are tooting. Everything's going at once, and I stand on top of the truck and finally we shoot off the big cannon. (*The crowd cheers, "Hurrah!"*) And the people, they walk right away . . . and don't even look back. (*The crowd is puzzled and disappointed. Pause.*) So then I realize, we are a little circus, right? Teeny, tiny circus, eh? A good circus, even great, but too small, too tiny. How could the people see us? How could they know we were alive? Here we are right under their feet and they couldn't even see us. It is grow up, my friends! Get big like the balloon here. Fill it up, Giuseppi! See my friends? That's how we must all grow up! It's time for a change . . . to grow! So!!! We have big acts, big animals, giant wagons, higher wires, bigger knives, fatter freaks. Then the people will come and will love us, and we will have the biggest balloon in the world! (*The crowd is wildly happy, cheering in many languages. Giuseppi accidentally lets the balloon escape, and it sails around until it is completely deflated and collapses on the floor. The crowd does not see this and continues to prance about. They exit hurriedly to prepare the big acts. Segue into "Tribute to Flight."*)

Scene ix   The Big Act and
the Old-Fashioned Man

*The circus people enter, a few at a time, with a flurry of activity —
dressing, arranging one another's costumes, readying themselves for
the "Tribute to Flight" tableau. When the music starts, they are in
place, "selling" the tableau with big smiles and waving fans.
Showgirls in capes and feathers flank a spaceship replica and there
are various bizarre apparitions scattered throughout the crowd: a
bird, a midget, two men in spacesuits and helmets holding Flash Gor-
don rocket posters, clowns, a pig, Lemo as an Air Force officer, a
dirigible, two acrobats waving huge ostrich feather fans, and the Tattooed Thin Man wearing a World War I flying ace outfit with helmet,
goggles, scarf, and cape. This tableau is an extravagantly tasteless
spectacle reminiscent of a commercially sponsored beauty pageant in
a discount store parking lot with searchlights and firecrackers. All
onstage pretend to watch an airplane pass overhead as the sound of a
jet engine is heard. Then the music fades and the people realize there
is no one to see their big show except the Old-Fashioned Man, who is
seated downstage, applauding. Lemo addresses the Old-Fashioned
Man.*

LEMO

(*haltingly*) Hello. We, ah, I, I'm sorry, but, this is our biggest act.
There is no people . . . You're people, of course . . . ONE
person is not like, ahhhh . . . We had colored smoke and my
daughter fly from the cannon . . . Ahhhhh, how's your popcorn? Here's a ticket. Here, have ten tickets for next week, I mean
for the next show . . . What can we do? We thought people were

67

coming . . . This is the biggest and best we ever had. I'm sorry . . .

OLD-FASHIONED MAN

Oh, no, no, that's all right. I really want to be in the circus. (*He dances around and addresses various circus folk.*) Oh, I've seen your act before . . . I've seen those used before . . . Well? (*Marvin throws swords at him, but they clatter harmlessly to the floor.*)

WILLIAM

I seen you before! I seen him before, I have, I seen him! I seen him all right. (*Approaching the Old-Fashioned Man, William loses his bluster and becomes meek and speechless.*)

DENISE

(*cursing at Lemo in French*) Toi, sot!!! (*Hélène cries, yells at Lemo, and spits at him. Nellie angrily throws her dress on the floor.*)

ZOLTAN

I want my money, Eugene, my money.

EUGENE

This is your big deal, eh, Lemo?

NORMA

(*to the Old-Fashioned Man*) Get outta here, you, you, you . . .

IRENE

You . . . Old-Fashioned Man! (*The frenzied crowd turns on the Old-Fashioned Man, and voices ad-lib: "He must be crazy!" "You nut!" "Get outta here!" "Mind your own business!"*)

MARVIN

That's right, mind your own business. You're probably the one messin' up things around here! (*He walks to the Old-Fashioned Man to kick him but gets a cramp in his leg and limps away moaning.*)

WILLIAM

I've seen him before. I seen him hangin' around here. (*Again William is confused and meek when he actually confronts the Old-Fashioned Man physically. The crowd yells: "Get outta here, get out, get out!"*)

LEMO

Ah! And besides, what can you do, eh? (*The Old-Fashioned Man performs dance steps that are idiosyncratic, unpredictable, and amusing.*)

EUGENE

Whaddaya think you're doin'? (*The Old-Fashioned Man stops, spins, and winks, teasing him.*)

OLD-FASHIONED MAN

How could YOU tell? (*Mystified, the circus folk mutter and question one another to see if anyone understands his remark.*)

LEMO

How could you tell? (*As the Old-Fashioned Man speaks the following lines, he darts about in the crowd, and various people in the circus pantomime the acts he describes. It is as if the people cannot stop themselves from tumbling and dancing, imitating animals, and behaving as though bewitched.*)

OLD-FASHIONED MAN

I've been in the circus, ohohoheehee! I used to have a trained seal act, twenty seals, a hundred rubber balls and horns . . . Can you see their flippers? Can you see 'em? Flap, flap, flap. When we were up above the ring, we used to do the triple, the triple, inside a wooden box, and land on top of an elephant. When the sides broke down, we all got down and played the violin with our toes. Hahahahaha . . . I've got a trained lion act that's guaranteed to do the job: Fifteen men line up and each puts a lion in his mouth while standing on his head. Can you stand on your head, son? On a camel? ONE hump? Two hundred thousand people saw that act. (*The astonished crowd gasps.*)

MARVIN

What was that act?

OLD-FASHIONED MAN

The Amphora Brothers and their dad, his name was Dan.

MARVIN

Oh yeah! I heard of them.

BARLEEN

Did you ever work with snakes?

OLD-FASHIONED MAN

Nope. But I WAS a snake for three years. Ho, ho, ho! I think I was a snake of yours and you never knew it. Did you know it? Hahahahahahaha, I've been with you, all of you. (*He dances among them, questioning and surprising them.*) You know me . . . I've been with you, all of you. You know me . . . I know you . . . Do you know me? . . . Look in a mirror . . . Look in your house . . . Look in a hat . . . Look in a trunk . . . I've been with you all . . . all of you . . . all the time . . . forever . . . The question is . . . are you with me? (*Immediately all are swept into a frenzied dance led by the Old-Fashioned Man. Their dance is wild, exultant, acrobatic, outrageous, and mysterious. They could be people in a religious revival meeting, all "filled with the spirit," or artists in the midst of the creative process, or mile runners nearing the finish line. Finally the exhausted dancers fall to the floor. The Old-Fashioned Man remains near the center, constantly on the move. There are no pauses between speeches; the pace of the dialogue quickens to match their excitement.*)

DENISE

Who are you?

OLD-FASHIONED MAN

Who are you?

NESTOR

Oh, come on.

MARIA

You have a name.

OLD-FASHIONED MAN

So do you. True?

NORMA

You remind me of someone, my dad or someone.

OLD-FASHIONED MAN

It could be, we'll see.

LEMO

Well, you're just great, just great, we have to say that. My, my. Say, you sure are.

OLD-FASHIONED MAN
Well, am I in?

EUGENE
In? You'll be the star attraction. You'll make us famous.

HELENE
Thank you for coming.

NINA
You'll be the star.

NORMA
And we'll be the most famous show in the world.

NESTOR
Let's get going.

ELAINE
Let's get rolling.

MARTIN
What do you say?

ERIC
Do you have an idea for an act?

OLD-FASHIONED MAN
Yep. (*He points to each person as he responds to their questions.*)

DELORES
Can I be in it?

OLD-FASHIONED MAN
Yep.

GREGA
Can I?

OLD-FASHIONED MAN
Yep.

BARLEEN
My snake, too?

OLD-FASHIONED MAN
Yep.

HELENE
My boys?

OLD-FASHIONED MAN
Yep.

EUGENE
   I'll announce.
OLD-FASHIONED MAN
   Good.
NELLIE
   You can juggle?
OLD-FASHIONED MAN
   You bet.
NINA
   Walk the wire?
OLD-FASHIONED MAN
   Yep.
GIUSEPPI
   You can talk to lions?
OLD-FASHIONED MAN
   Yep.
EMILE
   And do the triple?
OLD-FASHIONED MAN
   Yep.
MARVIN
   And eat fire?
OLD-FASHIONED MAN
   Yep.
ERIC
   Stand on your fingers?
OLD-FASHIONED MAN
   Yep.
MARIO
   Ride a bear?
OLD-FASHIONED MAN
   Yep.
WILLIAM
   And can you walk on air?
OLD-FASHIONED MAN
   Yep. (*The crowd gasps. He pauses.*) Well, I could try. (*The crowd laughs.*)

EUGENE
  We'll paint a big picture of you and all the acts.
ZOLTAN
  On an elephant.
MARTIN
  A big poster.
OLGA
  We'll all be famous.
MARIO
  Take his picture.
ANGELA
  No, take OUR picture. (*Marvin runs to downstage center with a camera and looks into the viewfinder. Everyone adjusts himself in a pose facing the audience, and Marvin snaps the picture.*)
NESTOR
  We'll start work tomorrow.
DENISE
  My dogs!
MARVIN
  My swords!
GIUSEPPI
  My high board!
OLGA
  Plates!
MARIO
  My stilts!
CAMILLE
  My ponies!
MARTIN
  My magic!
NORMA
  My fat! Oh no! (*She blushes and the crowd giggles.*)
OLD-FASHIONED MAN
  In the morning we'll start, with music. We'll be on the move. Now I'm tired, so good night. (*He reaches up and "turns off" the moon as if turning off a lamp. Blackout.*)

Scene x The Mint Lesson

Elaine is in her home, reading a newspaper and listening to the news. The scene is played in front of the closed proscenium curtains. A knock is heard.

ELAINE

Who is it? (*Jane and Emile hesitate in the shadows.*) Come in, come in. (*She indicates with a humorous step that they should dance in.*) You little Kinder . . . ha ha! (*They enter shyly and sit on either side of her.*) You ought to be in bed . . . such faces . . . Smile for old Elaine. (*She cajoles them into smiling.*) That's better! So, here, have a stick of gum, eh? Say, did you ever smell real mint? Oh, you can take the leaves and rub 'em between your fingers and smell good for the rest of the day. When I was a girl, we used to pick fresh mint in the summer and just smell it and smell it. But the funny thing is, you can never smell it hard enough to get all the sweetness out. That's the way everything ought to be . . . just no end to the sweetness . . . Well, you didn't come down here to listen to a mint lesson! (*They laugh.*) Well . . .

EMILE

Elaine . . . (*He pauses, finding it hard to speak, and looks to Jane for help.*)

ELAINE

Yes?

EMILE

We don't want to do the circus any more, Jane and I. We have talked and we want to stop, quit the circus. This man who came tonight . . . I do not think he is right . . . We do not wish to do the big act, the famous stuff, Elaine.

74

ELAINE
What? What do you mean?

JANE
We don't like it, I mean the circus and all. I can't stand it, I mean with the knives coming at a body all day long.

EMILE
Oui, oui, and always one-two-three-four all day to make the people happy!

ELAINE
But, the work? Work is good for you to do . . .

EMILE
Mama tells me all the time about Papa, the circus, Grandpa, all the old days! And she says I must do the stuff for the circus, but I do it, work hard, and then . . . When the people do applaud and cheer, I am not happy, because I don't care if I do the circus or not! And I wish . . . I was a million miles away!

JANE
And some nights, when I'm standing at the board, and Nestor tosses the knives around me, I think, what if one of them things missed and hit me? Who would cry? Nobody, 'cept Nestor and Emile . . . and you, Elaine. And then I wish I was a bird or somethin' so's I could just fly away, right in the middle of the show . . . right in the middle of the act . . . Whst . . . Whst . . . (*She imitates a bird taking off with her hands and they all laugh.*)

ELAINE
But where would you go? What would you do? Who would care for you, Jane?

JANE
I don't know 'cause I've never been no place else but the circus. But I'd sure like to find out . . . even for a minute.

EMILE
Elaine, what would happen to you, if you were to quit the circus?

ELAINE
(*adjusting her costume*) Oh . . . nothing . . . I'd be Elaine Schmitt . . . the lady . . . sitting wherever I was . . . on the

porch, or in a tree, or wherever I was . . . But for me now, I don't think about anything but the circus. That's what I know, that's what I am, I guess . . . You little ones, though, you got time to think . . . and time to fly . . . and that's good!! Now, every time I think about it, it's just too far down to the ground to even try. But you kids, go ahead, and when you get to the other side of the mountain . . . where it's all green . . . like the mint . . . let me know how it is. I might want to meet you there. (*She kisses them; they lean their cheeks against her knees and close their eyes.*) Now go to bed . . . (*crying*) My little birds . . . my little flowers . . . (*The Old-Fashioned Man appears behind her, unseen by them. Blackout.*)

Scene xi   "The trunks won't sink . . ."

The circus folk enter excitedly, a few at a time, until all are assembled together around the Old-Fashioned Man at center stage. They greet him as they enter: "Good morning!" "Well, we're ready!" "Here we are!" They talk and demonstrate bits of their acts to the Old-Fashioned Man and then go to another part of the stage to rehearse.

NORMA
    You know, I sure wish I could remember who you remind me of . . . My Grandpa, I think.
DENISE
    Here are my dogs.
OLD-FASHIONED MAN
    Good. (*Marvin shows him the board on which his swords hang. An axe hangs on the board along with more conventional swords, but Marvin offers no explanation of how it is to be swallowed.*)
MARVIN
    Many of these swords are rare.

OLD-FASHIONED MAN
Oh?

EUGENE
How do you want me to introduce the act? I speak Spanish too.

OLD-FASHIONED MAN
Well, so do I.

GERHARDT
Now, I can sing during your high wire act. I do "O Mein Papa" and "The Anniversary Waltz."

OLD-FASHIONED MAN
Do you know "In the Little Circus of My Mind"?

GERHARDT
No.

HELENE
And these are my boys, Emile and Gérard, and Lars Tils and . . . (*She introduces the acrobats to the Old-Fashioned Man and he shakes their hands.*)

ERIC
We can do a pyramid with you on top.

OLD-FASHIONED MAN
And a camel?

HELENE
Well . . .

IRENE
What will the freaks do?

WILLIAM
Do you have any tattoos?

OLD-FASHIONED MAN
A few. (*All begin to talk at once. The Old-Fashioned Man climbs a ladder at the center and gestures to hush them.*)

LEMO
Shush, shush. Let our friend talk . . . our old friend. Let him speak to us. Let's all get the spirit together. (*They become quiet. Silence.*) Well, we are ready. What do we do first? We want to do it right.

OLD-FASHIONED MAN
> (*speaking quietly and matter-of-factly as he eats an apple or a banana*) Throw it away. (*He continues to eat.*) Toss it out.

A VOICE
> What?

OLD-FASHIONED MAN
> Toss it out. Pack it up. Throw it away.

MARVIN
> Toss what?

EUGENE
> Something wrong?

NINA
> We can get something fixed.

LEMO
> We can get new equipment.

MARVIN
> We can buy new stuff.

WILLIAM
> What do you mean?

OLD-FASHIONED MAN
> I mean the circus. Put it in the trunks and drop it in the water . . . the sea. The trunks won't sink, you know.

MARVIN
> What? What do you mean? Is this supposed to be a joke?

OLD-FASHIONED MAN
> Nope.

EUGENE
> Well it's not funny.

NESTOR
> But what about the new act?

DENISE
> The dogs . . .

MARVIN
> The swords . . .

OLGA
> The plates . . .

GERARD
    My stilts . . .
MARTIN
    The cats . . .
HELENE
    My boys . . .
BARLEEN
    The snakes . . .
OLD-FASHIONED MAN
    Do you have what it takes to throw them out? I've seen your
    biggest show . . . I saw the act . . . the big poster, the rockets,
    and the smoke . . . No one came . . . It was a joke . . . Your
    balloon broke . . . and now, where do you all go? Pack the
    trunks, take down the poles, put the circus away, throw it into the
    sea and come with me. I told you it will float.
GIUSEPPI
    But where will we go?
HELENE
    We have no place.
DELORES
    It's all I know how to do.
NELLIE
    Me too.
FEDERICO
    We'll be lost.
CAMILLE
    What about you?
LEMO
    Yes, what about you?
OLD-FASHIONED MAN
    When all the circus is put into the sea, you climb onto the trunks.
    We'll go at night . . . tonight. You'll sail with me if you're not
    afraid of the water and the dark. And it's quite far out . . . to
    sea . . . before we get there . . .
MARVIN
    Where?

EUGENE
    You're crazy.

NESTOR
    I quit.

NINA
    Not me.

LEMO
    Shut up! (*to the crowd*) Besides, how could you tell? (*to the Old-Fashioned Man*) Right? (*The Old-Fashioned Man nods.*) Tonight then, did you say? OK, everybody, let's go, who knows! Madame Prinskaya, blow!!!! (*The band begins to play a sprightly song that diminishes into mood music creating night. A whistle blows, and they begin to dismantle the circus. Night falls and the rain comes. The new mood is somber and fearful. Distant voices ad-lib: "Roll 'em!" "Over here!" "Let down the ropes." Sounds of rain and wind are heard.*)

Scene xii   On the Wharf
in the Night Rain

The circus people huddle together in the rain and gloom; they are wearing slickers and holding umbrellas. Sounds of rain, wind, foghorns, and lapping water are heard throughout the scene. Some members of the circus approach a microphone held by a reporter and deliver testimonials as if in an "on the spot" television interview. During the testimonials large shipping trunks are carried onto the stage.

ERIC
    Eric Linds. I felt good . . . sorta good . . . before . . . in the daytime, this morning. But now that it's dark . . . I'm afraid.

LARS
Lars Tils. It's not that we're afraid of the dark exactly . . . We do the act in the dark, you know. It's now that our act is packed up . . . put away . . . and we're not sure what's coming ahead.

YVES
Yves Doussette. It's sort of like not being sure the wires are all tight and making sure they're OK before we go up. But tonight we can't check the wires. There aren't any wires to walk on tonight.

CAMILLE
Camille Deitz. I never have thought about doing anything but the circus. Have you?

MARIA
No.

CAMILLE
I mean I was born into it and it's what I know about. It's not a question for me of believing in the circus or not. It's that, in the show here, I know what's expected of me. I ride the horses and that's my part of it. I don't feel like doing anything else.

MARIA
Although you probably could.

CAMILLE
Even though I probably could.

FEDERICO
Federico Pollo. I'm pretty glad to be folding up this circus and going across the water. All I ever did was work while the other people, the quote artists, did the acts. For instance, one of my jobs was to hold the ropes while the girls did their routines. That's a . . . an important part, of course, but nobody who comes ever thinks so. Nobody says, "Hey, nice job on the ropes, Pollo!" 'Course if they did, I wouldn't think they meant it anyway.

IRENE
Irene Dress. When we get to the new place, I'm going to see to it that there's plenty room for my booth. Of course, I'm not a real fortune-teller . . . but people don't care. They like to have their palms read and to pretend that I know the future. And if the people like it . . . who cares if it's true or not. If it makes them

happy, then that's OK. But . . . I think I'm going to try for a bigger tent when we get there.

NINA

Nina Capek. I don't understand what's going on. I mean, why are we going? I love the circus and I think everybody does, even though the crowds were not coming. I believe it was just a bad time that will pass. I love my circus and I don't want to leave it and I think people who do are traitors . . . and I'm going to say so. I am not sure what to do, but I don't like leaving something that's been so good to me. I love my circus whether anybody likes it or not.

GREGA

Grega Kaputkeck. When I get there, I'm just going to lie there and rest . . . lie there!! I'll wonder what it would be like to just do nothing but be there. That's what a kid should be able to do. One time when we were between towns . . . one of the trucks broke down in the woods . . . We picked wild flowers until the tires were fixed, and it felt better than anything. Do you remember that?

ZOLTAN

Zoltan Capek. I'm going, but I don't like it. And if I fall into the water and drown, I don't care. This guy . . . I don't believe anything about him . . . He reminds me of someone that I hate.

BARLEEN

Barleen Toader. I work and work for six years to build an act into something and it's . . . it's fine for a while . . . I like it. Then the crowds started falling off and no one was coming and now what have I got to show for all the work? I don't understand . . . I don't know . . .

NELLIE

Nellie Jones. I know when we get there the people will like us. They've never seen a circus, I bet, and when they see our acts, our show, they'll just love us and flock to see us and applaud our stuff!! I'm going to check all the trunks and make sure all the equipment and costumes are on the raft. What about the animals, eh, Lemo? (*Eugene leaps onto the platform, aiming a gun at the Old-Fashioned Man.*)

OLD-FASHIONED MAN

And you with the gun . . . shoot me now, for when we're out to sea, the bullets will be too wet to fire. (*Eugene aims, ready to fire. Emile leaps to stop him; women scream and men shout and reach for Emile to protect him from being shot. Eugene fires but the Old-Fashioned Man is untouched. Gunshot sounds are created by the orchestra percussion.*) Thank you. (*All stare in disbelief when they see that the Old-Fashioned Man is not wounded.*) And now, retire to a trunk and we're off to hit a better target . . . and I'm no liar.

Scene xiii   The Sea Journey

The circus people, surrounded by their trunks, cling to a raft on the sea; it is night and the sea is tossed by a violent storm. Taped sound effects and the musical score combine to produce the atmosphere of a storm at sea. The circus people fall over one another as they are knocked about by the pitching of the raft; some are thrown through the air, and others are tossed from side to side. Lights flash, and voices moan and cry out. Finally the storm begins to diminish, and the exhausted people slump down and sleep. The lights fade out, then slowly come up on the sleeping group. It is now early morning, and the light is soft and golden. Gerhardt awakens first and begins singing for joy because they have survived the storm. One by one, others awaken, rouse their loved ones, and softly sing along with Gerhardt. Finally all are singing, in full voice, the "Song of the Sea." There are no lyrics; it is sung on "ah" or "la." The center platform moves slowly downstage toward the audience as warm sunshine envelops the circus people.

Scene xiv   The Farmers' Trunks

Lemo stands on a trunk and points into the audience.

LEMO

Look! Land! (*All rejoice. The platform moves back into place.
The circus people look about them, trying to see the land. The
lights gradually become white and blue, and the people hug
themselves as if they are chilly. They wear white shirts and dark
pants or shorts; their colorful circus clothes are gone. All but
Lemo and Eugene scramble off to explore. The Old-Fashioned
Man is not with them.*)

EUGENE

Look around, Lemo. Look around. What do you see, huh? What
do you see? Nothing.

ZOLTAN and NINA

(*rushing onstage*) Lemo, there's no water for the baby. No water.
(*Several other people straggle in, commenting that there are no
people — nothing — on the island.*)

LEMO

Well, let's open up the trunks. At least we can put up the tents.
(*Eugene goes to a trunk and opens the lid. It is filled with seed.*)

EUGENE

Lemo, these ain't even our trunks! These are full of seed. Not even
our trunks! (*They open other trunks and find plants, hoes, and
bags of water. The circus people enter on both sides of the stage,
excitedly bringing in plants and seeds. Someone has found water.
The stage is flooded with warm light. Everyone begins working,
planting, laughing, and talking excitedly with one another.*)

84

LEMO
We don't need a tent. Look, look, so what if we aren't the biggest circus, eh?

ELAINE
Oh, Emile, look at you now, eh? Emile, the farmer. And look at the mama, too! She plants the seeds again . . . together you work. And you must make your papa smile. You know that for sure, eh, Gérard! (*Calling to Gérard, she motions for him to water the ground. Then Hélène and her two sons stand arm in arm, surveying their work.*) And I think things come up mint this time . . . (*At last they all sit back, exhausted but elated. Marvin enters with one of the circus poles, which has started to sprout leaves, and gives it to Emile at the center of the stage. Emile holds the pole firmly before him.*)

LEMO
Maybe we should be here. We have water, and seeds and rakes and . . . who knows? Hey, Eugene, we can be the greatest farmers of the world, ah? Hahahahahaha! (*All the circus people talk and work happily together. Pepper begins to juggle a hoe with one hand and William instructs him, telling him how to do it better. Grega juggles seed bags. Emile and Gérard perform stunts on the circular platform at the center. The adults give instructions to the children. Everyone is smiling and laughing, and their energy soars to a peak. Then the lights fade to a blackout, during which all the actors exit. Mottled green lights come up and linger on the stage, which is now filled with greenery.*)

How Could You Tell? The clowns in the circus walk-around. (Photograph courtesy of the Minneapolis Institute of Arts.)

How Could You Tell? The showgirls in the circus walk-around. (Photograph courtesy of the Minneapolis Institute of Arts.)

How Could You Tell? Tableau: Tribute to flight. (Photograph courtesy of the Minneapolis Institute of Arts.)

How Could You Tell? "I've been with you all . . . all of you . . . all the time . . forever." (Photograph courtesy of the Minneapolis Institute of Arts.)

The Cookie Jar

MOTHER MARY
The bird in flight seeks other wings;
The frog wants more singers on the lily pad.
The little old worm likes company, oh, yeah,
Just look into a fisherman's can!

Dedicated to the memory of Mahalia Jackson

The Cookie Jar was first produced by the Children's Theatre Company of the Minneapolis Society of Fine Arts in March 1972. The script was edited by Linda Walsh Jenkins with the assistance of Carol K. Metz.

Cast of Characters

Bubble	A young boy
Winde	The presence of God, the Holy Spirit
Black-Eyed Pea	A teenaged black girl
Old Glue Needle, Wet Paint Bill, and Mother Mary .	Inhabitants of the Matchbox House

Members of the Stale Cake Company:

Daddy Tutti-Fruit Hat..	A combination of ringmaster, disc jockey, and used car salesman
Diana Dumbstrut	A brassy blond cheerleader, the advertising world's sexy female
Dorothy Doughie	An aging parody of Shirley Temple as a child star
Oreo Cookie Man	A white man in blackface with an Afro wig
Captain Steal..........	A hippie rock star with a wooden leg
Electric Piggybank Man	No one knows if he is a pig that turned into a man or a man who turned into a pig. He rides a tricycle which pulls the Dream Wagon, a vehicle vaguely resembling the small cart used by an ice cream vendor. The Dream Wagon contains gadgets, props, and toys.
People of Cookie Land ...	Approximately twenty children, teenagers, and adults

Sequence of Scenes

Notes on the Play

The people of Cookie Land have lost all their old recipes for living a simple, happy life. The Stale Cake Company convinces them that the reason for living is "to get everything you can, and the Stale Cake Company is here to help you get it." The plot of the play is essentially melodramatic: The villains (the Stale Cake Company) try to beguile the people of Cookie Land with worthless trinkets and gadgets, but in the end their mischief is foiled by the Matchbox House people (representing the forces of good) who lead the Stale Cake Company and the people of Cookie Land to the good life at the Matchbox House. There the Stale Cake Company members are converted and shed their makeup and gaudy clothes for simple white aprons and chef's hats. In the final communion scene everyone shares lemonade and a giant homemade cookie. The color and continuity of the story rely heavily on Roberta Carlson's musical score, which combines elements of ragtime, rock, gospel songs, blues, swing, and boogie-woogie in an instrumentation for bass, drums, trumpet, saxophone, clarinet, flute, guitar, piano, and organ.

The setting is a gigantic mixing bowl that fills the stage. The side of the bowl toward the audience is represented only by the rim, which soars and curves from one side of the proscenium to the other. The rim is supported by a ladder and a giant matchstick. The surface of the bowl is painted to look like an old fence or a billboard covered with ragged remnants of old posters and paintings. At upstage right the bowl is partially cut away; in the "Famine" scene this section is backlighted with red to create an inferno effect. A rope ladder and wooden pegs are affixed to the surface of the bowl to allow children to climb on it. Black velours are hung upstage of the bowl. The openings on either side of the bowl are curtained with red cloth that is gathered to suggest entrances to a circus tent.

The Matchbox House is a giant matchbox lying on its side. The drawer of the matchbox slides across the stage to reveal a jumble of matches from which hang clothing, lamps, pots, and pans. A slide behind the matchbox lid provides one means of entering the house. The only furniture for the Matchbox House consists of an overstuffed armchair, a painter's easel, and an ironing board that has been made into a piano keyboard. In the 1973 production of the play the company substituted a giant umbrella for the matchbox. The umbrella lay on its side on a rolling platform, its handle toward the audience, and the household was arranged on the platform in the cavelike shelter of the umbrella. The umbrella proved to be an efficient stage device, especially for touring purposes.

The costumes are contemporary. The Stale Cake Company's costumes are meant to be as garish and tasteless as their routines and their behavior. Mother Mary, Bubble, Black-Eyed Pea, Wet Paint Bill, and Old Glue Needle dress in clothes that are timeless, simple, and unpretentious.

Prologue   Children Playing

As the musicians in the orchestra play a lyrical jazz set, small children crawl, climb, wander, and play on the stage, swinging on ropes and climbing along the rim of the mixing bowl. Mother Mary enters and sits with a storybook in a big armchair. The children sit at her feet, and she reads to them. The mottled lighting and the music create a dreamlike atmosphere; the audience cannot hear Mother Mary over the music. It is as though the audience were privy to a memory of the scene.

Scene i   "Bake a Cookie for Me!"

Theme: "Bake a Cookie for Me!" The lights change to a warm pool on Mother Mary and the children.

MOTHER MARY

Once upon a time in a place called Cookie Land, there lived an old lady. But afore I tell you about this old lady, I'm goin' to tell you sumpin' about Cookie Land. Now they called this place Cookie Land 'cause it was the only thing they had for to live on, was cookies! 'Course they had every kind of cookies in this land, for instance, they had . . . ooohh, ahhhh, lettuce cookies, mashed potatoes cookies, grits cookies, and so on. They had winter stockin' cookies, so they didn't get cold in the feet. Now then, anyway, this old lady went to the kitchen to get a coconut macaroon cookie that she had baked a long time ago. But when she got up in the cupboard by way of an old rickety ladder, built for her by her husband before he died — a loony death — out on the front lawn in the middle of a hailstorm, well, anyway, this tired old lady . . .

CHILD

A witch?

MOTHER MARY

No, not a witch, just a tired old lady . . . anyhow, she went to the cupboard and reached into the cookie jar, and all she found was a hard-as-a-rock raisin and a dead mouse.

CHILD

What happened?

MOTHER MARY

She died. She starved to death in three days because she forgot the recipe. Some kids in the neighborhood found her dead on the kitchen floor. And written in flour under the sink was this message: "Bake a cookie for me!" . . . Did you like that? (*The children smile and nod. She hugs them, and they talk quietly as the lights fade.*)

Scene ii The Stale Cake
Company and Bubble

The lights come up on Winde, sweeping and singing in the street. He speaks to the audience.

WINDE

Hello. This is the main street of Cookie Land, and I am in charge of sweeping the crumbs off of the pavement. But occasionally one or two slip by me . . . Like now! (*Boogie theme: "The Wooden Spoon Hop." The inhabitants of Cookie Land and the members of the Stale Cake Company make their entrances in a choreographed sequence. Most are teenagers dressed in contemporary style but not exaggeratedly so. They wear gold paper crowns, many chew gum, some wave cheerleaders' pompoms. Their gestures and movements possess the artless vulgarity seen in some television choreography. The Cookie Land people begin to arrive and to greet the Stale Cake Company. The Electric Piggybank Man pushes in Diana Dumbstrut, who rides on a workman's dolly; she is swathed in cellophane and is flanked by a giant plastic fork and spoon. She looks like a cheap plastic doll sold at a discount store. She steps through the cellophane, blows a whistle, does a drum majorette's backbend, then dances to the side. The people scream and cheer. Dorothy Doughie and the Oreo Cookie Man enter. They do brief dances that are associated with their roles throughout the play and join Diana Dumbstrut. Captain Steal enters with a huge poster which he unfurls. It reads "Stale Cake Company," with the lettering in the style of a Coca-Cola sign. Two girls carry the sign upstage and hold it there to frame the action at center stage as Captain Steal joins the others. Finally, Daddy Tutti-Fruit Hat enters and displays a sign that reads "Cookie Trip — Win!! Just Bake It." He strides over to the assembled crowd.*)

DADDY TUTTI-FRUIT HAT
   (*in the oily voice of a disc jockey*) Hi, kids!
CHILDREN
   Hi!
DADDY TUTTI-FRUIT HAT
   How's every little thing?
CHILDREN
   Fine!
DADDY TUTTI-FRUIT HAT
   Far out! You know, you kids really take the cake! (*As he says this, he lifts his whip above his head and freezes at the end of the sentence. Everyone onstage freezes except Bubble. The lights dim on them, leaving only a pool of light on Bubble, who is seated downstage on the rim of the bowl-world. A flute is heard.*)
BUBBLE
   Hello. You know, come to think of it . . . I am not too happy with the way things are in my life, and I'm not very old yet either, nine or so. Yesterday I made this little flute out of sticks . . . it doesn't really play, but it's like I saw in a picture once . . . I wish I played the flute or something . . . I have a snapshot of my Uncle Steve playing the fiddle at a picnic but that was before me and I never heard it . . . Anyway, so much is happening to confuse a person these days . . . certain kinds of birds dying out, people building fences in their yards to keep out something. Kids fighting over who's got the best color . . . bike or not. My dad said I couldn't plant corn and sunflowers in the backyard 'cause it was too much trouble and tracked in dirt, my ma said . . . I think I'll dress up in a leaf suit and climb up in a tree and stay there, dressed in my leaf suit, forever . . . at least the wind and I'd have a lot to agree upon. (*The lights come up suddenly as the others onstage snap back into action.*)
DADDY TUTTI-FRUIT HAT
   All right, kids!
ELECTRIC PIGGYBANK MAN
   (*pointing to Bubble and oinking for Daddy Tutti-Fruit Hat's attention*) Oink! Oink! Oink!

DADDY TUTTI-FRUIT HAT

Heeeyyy! Heeeyyyy! (*He goes to Bubble.*) What are ya doin' up
there? Come on down here, fast! (*Bubble jumps into his arms.*)
What do you need, huh? What do you need? (*Daddy Tutti-Fruit
Hat shoves Bubble into the group of children.*)

SHEILA

Hey, what's the matter with you? Didn't you know the Stale Cake
Company was in town?

MATT

Yeah, man, they're neato, keeno!

RICKY

They're the coolest, man!

BARRY

What's the matter with you?

KIM

Yeah, get with it.

DADDY TUTTI-FRUIT HAT

All right, kids, here it is! The Portable Key Toast Hat! (*He puts a
toaster-hat device on his head, pulls a cord, and plastic wedges
pop up. The children scream and cheer.*) Only $7.95 in toy
departments everywhere. Put it right on your head, pull the little
strap down. Pops 'em right up, huh? Is that beautiful? Is that far
out or what?

DIANA DUMBSTRUT

You can have a hot waffle any time when you wear this hat.

DADDY TUTTI-FRUIT HAT

All right, sweetheart, step right up here! (*to the others*) Get back!
All right, you . . . (*He pulls one of the girls from the crowd.*)
What's your name, darling?

BRIDGET

Bridget!

DADDY TUTTI-FRUIT HAT

How old are you, Bridget?

BRIDGET

Eleven. (*She squirms and waves to her friends; she is chewing gum
and her speech is barely intelligible.*)

DADDY TUTTI-FRUIT HAT
  Eleven . . . Bridget, would you like to pull the Portable Key Toast cord?
BRIDGET
  Yeah!
DADDY TUTTI-FRUIT HAT
  Go ahead, give it a little tug. (*Bridget barely touches it.*) That's enough! (*He pushes her away.*) All right, Bridget, for your test, I'm going to see if you can do the "Wooden Spoon Hop"! All right, let's everyone snap your fingers and help Bridget out! (*The children snap their fingers in rhythm. Bridget does an absurd dance step reminiscent of the "Mashed Potato." The children yell "Sad!" "Far out!" and similar slang jargon. Daddy Tutti-Fruit Hat stops Bridget's dance.*) Isn't she far out? Here's a couple of tickets to the big show, sweetheart! OK, guys and gals, boys and girls, swingers! Here we go with another far out rendition of the Stale Cake Company theme song! (*Theme: "The Stale Cake Company." As Daddy Tutti-Fruit Hat sings, the Stale Cake Company and the children sing a 1950s rock "oooohhhh!" background. They sway in the dance style of the 1950s.*)
  It's the real thing, it's the true thing,
  It's a love thing, it's a good thing,
  It's a God thing, it's a stale thing!
STALE CAKE COMPANY
  Lemme tell ya!
DADDY TUTTI-FRUIT HAT
  You can get it and we're here to tell you how!
STALE CAKE COMPANY
  Oh, ya need it!
DADDY TUTTI-FRUIT HAT
  You can get it and it's waiting right here,
  If you only come and . . .
DADDY TUTTI-FRUIT HAT and STALE CAKE COMPANY
  Buy, buy, buy!
  (*The children cheer and whistle.*)

DADDY TUTTI-FRUIT HAT

Far out. That was really beautiful, you guys. I'm going to take off the Portable Key Toast Hat and put back on the Daddy Tutti-Fruit Hat, because it's serious time now, kids . . . (*underscore: "The Stale Cake Company"*) I'm going to tell you a little story, a story of truth and meaning for modern man in these troubled times, and you boys and girls, too . . . I'm going to tell you of a woman who came to me in dire distress. She did not know what to do. Her life was a shambles, her marriage was on the rocks, her husband drank heavily because of an accident at work, and her daughter was a bummer at school. *And* she had just lost her blouse. She did not know what to do. She came to me and she said, "Daddy Tutti-Fruit Hat, I do not know what to do, but I read your ad in this comic book and I just hope that you can help me out." And I said, "My dear, I am Daddy Tutti-Fruit Hat, are I not?" And she said, "Yes, you are." And I said, "My dear, here you take this, free of charge on a thirty-day free trial, money-back guarantee, the Stale Cake Company's very own Franges Dober Flutter, $11.95 at toy departments everywhere (*speaking rapidly*) requires seven-Eveready-Triple-A-Penlight-batteries-batteries-not-included." Well, she took it home and the next day she came back to me and she said, "Daddy Tutti-Fruit Hat, God came to me last night, and He said, 'I put you on this earth to get everything you can, and the Stale Cake Company is there to help you get it!'" From that day on, she got everything that she could. She went downtown and she got and she got and she bought and she bought and she got and she bought and she bought and she got. Her husband got his job back! (*The members of the Stale Cake Company and a few of the children call out as if in response to a revival testimonial: "Yeah!" "Tell 'em!" "Right on!"*) He stopped drinking. She found her lost blouse. And her daughter became far out.

ALL

(*yelling*) Far out!

DADDY TUTTI-FRUIT HAT

Her daughter became right on!

ALL

Right on!

DADDY TUTTI-FRUIT HAT

Her daughter became . . . Miss Diana Dumbstrut, the Girl with the Golden Goose! Here she is, the living testimony! (*Percussion accompanies Daddy Tutti-Fruit Hat's introduction of Diana Dumbstrut. Daddy Tutti-Fruit Hat steps aside and gestures toward Diana Dumbstrut in the manner of an announcer introducing a nightclub act. The children shriek and cheer as she steps into the spotlight. She leans back into a drum majorette pose, nearly falls, then stands and poses. She is the dumb blond stereotype: She cannot talk very well, her voice is shrill, she twitches, her eggbeater baton slips over her eye, and her fake eyelashes make her appear cross-eyed. She constantly wears a Miss America smile and keeps glancing over at Daddy Tutti-Fruit Hat to see how she is doing.*)

DIANA DUMBSTRUT

I was no one . . . and nobody knew who I was. I had nothing, and then I met Daddy Tutti-Fruit Hat and the Stale Cake Company, and they told me this, which I will remember to this very day. They said to me, "Go out and get. Get all you can!" And so I got and I got and I bought and I bought. I bought my suit, and the Franges Dober Flutter, and my baton, and now, I am . . . Diana Dumbstrut! (*All cheer.*)

DADDY TUTTI-FRUIT HAT

Isn't she far out! (*All cheer.*) Isn't she right on!

ALL

Right on! (*Diana Dumbstrut returns to the Stale Cake Company. Daddy Tutti-Fruit Hat takes the spotlight again.*)

DADDY TUTTI-FRUIT HAT

Thanks very much, Diana, you're a sweetheart. All right, boys and girls, I know you're anxious to try out your own Portable Key Toast Hat and your own Franges Dober Flutter! (*The children cheer after each item is mentioned.*) And your recipe for the Mini Cookie! (*He ad-libs the names of other products.*) But first I'm going to ask Diana Dumbstrut, the Girl with the Golden Goose, to lead us down the street in a parade. (*Theme: "The Stale Cake Company." They march out with Diana Dumbstrut leading. Bubble is left sitting on the stage, watching them go. Winde comes onstage from the audience, sweeping.*)

WINDE

Hey, what you got there?

BUBBLE

It's a little flute, but it's not real.

WINDE

Let me see it. Did you make it yourself?

BUBBLE

Yeah.

WINDE

That's pretty good! You know something? You're going to learn to play that flute someday.

BUBBLE

I hope so. (*Boogie theme: "The Wooden Spoon Hop." Daddy Tutti-Fruit Hat and several children dance across the stage. Daddy Tutti-Fruit Hat gestures for Bubble to join them, but Bubble just watches. The lights fade down.*)

Scene iii   Bubble and Winde

As the lights come up slowly, Bubble runs onstage with an umbrella, climbs the ladder hurriedly, and sits on the rim of the bowl-world downstage. Thunder. Offstage, a voice calls faintly. Bubble opens the umbrella and curls up underneath it to sing and daydream. A girl is leaning against the proscenium, and a boy is sitting, his chin in his hands and his elbows propped on his knees, on a rung of the ladder. The girl sings with Bubble, and the boy, getting up and moving away from the ladder, speaks some of the lines of the song to emphasize the images.

BUBBLE and GIRL
>> (*singing*)
>> Once I was a bubble . . .

BOY
> Once I was a bubble . . .

BUBBLE and GIRL
>> (*singing*)
>> On the rushing water stream . . .

BOY
> On the rushing water stream . . .

BUBBLE and GIRL
>> (*singing*)
>> A sailing ball . . .

BOY
> A sailing ball . . .

BUBBLE and GIRL
>> (*singing*)
>> A magic sea ship,
>> A window for a fish.

BOY
> . . . A window for a fish.

(*Winde enters on a bicycle during the song. He wears a farmer's straw hat and carries a sprinkling can in the bicycle basket. He rides between the girl and the boy to the ladder and joins in the singing.*)

BUBBLE, GIRL, and WINDE
> (*singing*)
>> We played a while, then rolled and tumbled,
>> The bubble and the wave,
>> Two glass clowns from a water show,
>> Two clear spring days . . .

(*The boy who spoke wanders away, lost in his own daydreams now, and exits.*)

>> Each juggling river drops
>> On the tips of wet fingers,
>> When I awoke, the river dry, its bed my own,
>> But I, my hair still salt wet, my pillow

Still dream sweet.
(*The girl drifts away and exits.*)

WINDE

That's quite a story.

BUBBLE

Yes, but how did you know it, too? You sang right along with me.

WINDE

Well, you know, I think I had that same dream myself when I was your age. In fact, I still have it now . . . some days.

BUBBLE

Gosh! Who are you, anyway?

WINDE

Today I'm taking care of the flowers, tryin' to bring a little sunshine and a little soft rain to them. (*During this exchange two young girls bring potted plants to Winde, who examines the plants, waters them carefully, and shares a smile with each girl. The girls exit.*) They could use it, you know. Boy, this summer's been hot.

BUBBLE

Wow! It sure has. You're a gardener, I suppose.

WINDE

Oooohhh . . . some days.

BUBBLE

I'd like that job . . . I think.

WINDE

Some days . . . you probably would. Try it sometime.

BUBBLE

Yeah. But I thought I saw you working in the street, yesterday, sweeping.

WINDE

Some days.

BUBBLE

Oh! I see . . . part-time here and part-time there, sort of . . . You work part-time. You've got more than one job. Part-time here and part-time there.

WINDE

Well . . . that's one way to put it . . . or maybe all over the place . . . a little bit . . . all the time.

BUBBLE

Hmmm. (*He thinks about it.*) What's your name?

WINDE

(*pause*) Wind . . . -e; Winde.

BUBBLE

Well, 'bye, Winde, gotta go home now. There's a robin building a nest in the backyard in our hedge. So anyway, I got this box of string and stuff that I'm goin' to throw in the grass . . . in case he needs it. 'Bye! (*He blows on the stick flute. Suddenly it works and he is astonished. Flute.*) Wow! (*He heads down the ladder and says "Wow!" again. He jumps on Winde's bike and rides off blowing his flute as the orchestra picks up the fluting and makes a transition into wind sounds.*)

Scene iv   Jivin'

Theme: "Jivin' Boogie." This scene was improvised by the black teenagers of the Children's Theatre Company, and it is offered as an example, not as a set script. The teenagers created the dialogue and jokes out of their own shared vocabulary and references. The names used were those of the actors. The setting is a jive session among friends.

KIM

Here's the way Mr. Johnson walks: he's a teacher at our school. Here's the way he walks, tryin' to walk the way we do. Chicka boom, chicka boom, chicka boom boom boom . . . (*Laughter. Everyone talks at once as Kim minces across the stage. Kim mimics Mr. Johnson.*) Uh, give me five, sister. (*The teenagers laugh; each tries to top the other.*)

ARTIE

Guess what, Garry, yesterday in school we had a vote . . .

GARRY

So . . .

ARTIE

You won.

GARRY

Won what?

ARTIE

Out!

GARRY

Out?

ARTIE

O-U-T! (*All laugh and gesture freely throughout the scene, appreciating one another's jokes; friendly battles develop.*)

KEVIN

Speaking of Garry, I saw Garry walkin' down the street, and these other black people were walkin' the other way. So Garry started sayin', "Black is beautiful! Black is beautiful!" And one of the black dudes stopped, looked at Garry, and said, "Wait, we got to talk about this one!"

GARRY

Well, did Kevin tell you that him and his brothers were going to get on the bus the other day? They didn't have the fare to pay so the driver took them to the back . . .

ALL

To the back!

GARRY

Put some paper down . . .

ALL

Put some paper down . . .

GARRY

And put them on some chairs and said, "Don't make a dirty pit back here." In other words, you are a dog!

DAVID

Wait, everybody, one of these days I am going to be rich!

ALL

Sad!

DAVID

I'm going to have a rich car, a rich house, a rich woman, and a rich phone. And I'm going to call you, and you, and maybe you two over there, and I'm going to dial and say, "Ding a ling."

ALL

Hello!

DAVID

I'm sorry, but you got the wrong number — and I'm going to hang up!

NANCE

When you get rich! Honey, you're so poor now, you can't even afford nothing free!

GARRY

Wait a minute, everybody, shut up! When I get rich, like he just said, I'm going to walk in front of the TV set, and the band will be playin' behind me. And I'm going to tell you (*looking at Kim*) to turn your set off, 'cause I'm too good to be looked at and might blind your eyes.

KIM

Honey, I hate to say it, but you're going to have to pay them to get on that TV set.

GARRY

They've got to pay you to get off!!! Cockroach face! (*The "Jivin' Boogie" theme picks up underneath.*)

KIM

Yeah, well, I went over to Garry's house, which they purchased through S and H Gold Bond stamps. And I went up to the house, which looked like somebody's back alley. I walked up to the refrigerator . . .

NANCE

Ah-ah . . . icebox, honey.

DAVID

No, you mean cooler.

KEVIN

No way . . . you mean picnic basket.

KIM

I walked up to the picnic basket, looked in, and I saw cockroaches inside, dancin' around, and they had signs. You know why? 'Cause they were on strike. And do you know what they were doing? They were singing; here's what they were singing . . .

ALL

(*singing*)
    We done overcome,
    We sho' had some fun . . .

GARRY

That's all right, Miss Tons of Fun. I came over to your house, which you got at Pay Less Shoes. Knocked on the door, which fell apart afterwards, and a cockroach came and said, "Hat and coat, please." I said, "Sho', honey, but where's your master?" And them cockroaches were fat and greasy.

KEVIN

Hold on, everybody, I got a joke. See there was this black man and this white man on the bus . . .

DAVID

Wait, Kevin, I think I figured out why you tell so many racial jokes . . . 'Cause you *are* a racial joke. (*Kevin and David start arguing; Nance stops them.*)

NANCE

Ah, be quiet and listen to me, Kevin. Your racial jokes are so funky that when you moved into your neighborhood the neighbors' grass died!

KEVIN

Yeah, you know what I heard? I heard that if you put your brain on a razor blade, it would look like a BB rolling down a four-lane highway. Now beat that!

KIM

Oh, Garry, guess what . . .

GARRY

Shut up, Big Lips!

KIM

Y'all heard of banjo eyes, have ya? Well, you're looking at banjo lips. Why, his lips is so big that his mother had to make him a lip case, and on the cover she put his nickname.

NANCE

What was it, honey?

KIM

"Chopper" . . . Not only that, but at night he has to wear a lip brace, so his lips won't fall out of the bed.

GARRY

Honey, I hate to tell you that your nickname is Rotunda Lips, Bongo Lips, Raw Steak Lips . . . (*He ad-libs.*) Your friends just said that you had two big disaster areas on the lower part of your face. Meaning your big baggy watermelon lips. (*He changes the subject.*) Now show me what you've got in that sack.

KIM

I went downtown the other day, by ghetto express . . .

GARRY

Your family owns it.

KIM

Yeah! That's why you walk so much. Hey, I heard that blonds have more fun . . .

NANCE

Who told you that?

KIM

Well, I decided to cash in on some of that fun that I have been missing out on. (*She takes a blond wig from the sack and begins strutting across the stage. Garry snatches the wig, puts it on, and does an imitation of a white blond "swinger." Others begin dancing. Garry throws the wig on the floor and dances in up-to-date black style. Everyone joins in, laughing and talking, until the music stops abruptly.*) There was a soul food dinner at our school the other day.

ARTIE

What did they have?

KIM
>   Black-eyed peas.

ALL
>   And do you know what them black-eyed peas was?

GARRY
>   Pork 'n' beans burnt on one side. (*The music resumes. The
>   teenagers dance and continue "jivin'," then they turn upstage and
>   dance toward the wall of the bowl. Black-Eyed Pea enters, carry-
>   ing her parasol, and walks through them to a pool of light at the
>   center.*)

Scene v   Black-Eyed Pea

There is a clash of cymbals; the music stops and the teenagers freeze.

BLACK-EYED PEA
>   Yeah, things began to change and I stopped hanging around with
>   those other kids, and when girls would call me up I'd say I was
>   sick or somethin'. Instead I go up on the roof by the chimney and
>   just sit up there and listen. (*The other teenagers speak lines out of
>   the darkness upstage.*)

GARRY
>   To what?

BLACK-EYED PEA
>   I heard this voice saying or kind of singing . . . all the
>   time . . . !

STEPHANIE
>   So?

BLACK-EYED PEA
>   So . . . one night I went out and I looked for it. It was late,
>   morning, in fact . . . I guess, but still dark . . . my feet wet
>   and catching sick, maybe . . . So I put on this old pair of yellow
>   overshoes, I don't know whose they were, they were in the

garage . . . they looked like (*underscore: "Sweet Jesus, Precious Savior"**) fireman's or fishing boots or something . . . I was walking in the street . . . They sounded like a tin bells machine or I don't know . . . When I walked, I made little rhythms as I went . . . and I remember humming "Sweet Jesus, Precious Savior," slushing out a rubber dance against the curb. (*The others softly hum the song.*)

STEPHANIE
What happened?

BLACK-EYED PEA
I never saw anybody else. It was like I was walking through a model or something . . . you know? . . . and no sound except the buckles playing on my boots. No cars . . . no dogs . . . no doors shutting . . . no whistles . . . only . . . just me . . . my voice . . . my breath . . . my feet crunch . . . my pockets . . . my parade walk . . . music only. And the long low cry, cooing . . . begging . . . "Come on home, child . . . come on home . . . come on home to the kitchen table." (*She sings to the tune of "Sweet Jesus, Precious Savior."*)

> Come on home
> To the kitchen, kitchen table . . .
> Come on . . .

(*Bubble enters, carrying his umbrella. He walks to her and stands watching her.*)

BUBBLE
To the kitchen table?

BLACK-EYED PEA
Yeah.

BUBBLE
Did this voice say anything about cookies?

BLACK-EYED PEA
Cookies! What you mean cookies? What ya talkin'! . . . Cookies!

BUBBLE
Well, you said "kitchen," didn't you?

*Music on page 168.

BLACK-EYED PEA
Yeah.
BUBBLE
You bake cookies in the kitchen, don't you?
BLACK-EYED PEA
Yeah. Here I am talkin' voices and singin' and you're talkin' cookies! I'll bake *your* cookie! (*laughing*) What's your name, puppy? What's your name, puppy chil'?
BUBBLE
Bubble.
BLACK-EYED PEA
Bubble! Your name?
BUBBLE
Yes.
BLACK-EYED PEA
You mean people call you by "Bubble"? (*She laughs.*)
BUBBLE
Yes.
BLACK-EYED PEA
Sad! (*out of her laughter*) I'm a black-eyed pea.
BUBBLE
What?
BLACK-EYED PEA
Are you deaf?
BUBBLE
What?
BLACK-EYED PEA
I said, are you deaf?
BUBBLE
What?
BLACK-EYED PEA
He's deaf! I said, you're the bubble, I'm the black-eyed pea!
BUBBLE
Wow! You're the first other person I ever met without a regular name. How'd ya get it? Is that your real name?

BLACK-EYED PEA
> 'Course not. Is Bubble yours?

BUBBLE
> Well, no!

BLACK-EYED PEA
> Well then, hush up and shut your face . . . (*She laughs.*)
> Hey . . . you play that thing? (*She points to his flute.*)

BUBBLE
> No! Well . . . (*He remembers the sound.*)

BLACK-EYED PEA
> Huh?

BUBBLE
> Well, I guess so.

BLACK-EYED PEA
> Well, play it! (*He blows on it. Flute sounds are heard.*) Sit down.
> I'm going to tell you a little story here. (*Theme: "Black-Eyed Pea."* Black-Eyed Pea sings the verses and choruses with great freedom and ease.*)

> *In summer when the air is heavy breath,*
> *And the butterfly can float upon its back,*
> *I used to hide deep in the pea patch*
> *And listen to the warm ground breathing back.*
> *And I'd wonder how the earth it got so black.*

> *Black-Eyed Pea, Black-Eyed Pea,*
> *If you're wonderin' where this song comes from,*
> *Then take a look at me.*
> (Repeat refrain.)

> *In summer I'd pick the blossoms from the pea vine*
> *And wind them through my hair.*
> *And then I'd scoop the black dirt up*
> *And toss it everywhere.*
> *I musta been blessing the pea patch*
> *'Cause it was quiet and holy there.*

*Music on page 169.

Black-Eyed Pea, Black-Eyed Pea,
If you're wonderin' where this song comes from,
Then take a look at me.
(Repeat refrain.)

Later on in the summer, when the peas were ready to eat,
I went down to the pea patch, the air was smelling sweet.
I gazed into the garden and there to my surprise,
The pea patch I saw before my eyes was a pea patch in dis-
guise.
Instead the leaves were silver wings and the pods were
slippers fine.
And the waters from the rain before were jewels upon the
vine.
I was the ruler of the kingdom, my subjects were so fine.
If you want a favor from me, just ask me any time.

Black-Eyed Pea, Black-Eyed Pea,
If you're wonderin' what to call me,
Just call me "Your Majesty."
(Repeat refrain.)

(*laughing*) No. I made that up. But anyway, I was always out in
the back patch. So that's what they called me after a while, all the
time, Black-Eyed Pea. That's how I got my name.

BUBBLE

Black-Eyed Pea . . .

BLACK-EYED PEA

Yes, Bubble . . .

BUBBLE

Can I be your friend?

BLACK-EYED PEA

Well, I guess you'd better be. (*They laugh. The "Bubble and*
Black-Eyed Pea" vamp begins. Bubble and Black-Eyed Pea walk
in place in tempo through the next exchange, until the thunder
sounds. They walk facing the audience like a vaudeville comic
duo in a patter routine.)

BUBBLE
Black-Eyed Pea, do you like cars?
BLACK-EYED PEA
Nope.
BUBBLE
Not even big long shiny red ones that go fast?
BLACK-EYED PEA
Nope.
BUBBLE
Do you like . . . TV?
BLACK-EYED PEA
Nope.
BUBBLE
To sing?
BLACK-EYED PEA
Yup.
BUBBLE
Dancin'?
BLACK-EYED PEA
Yup.
BUBBLE
Doin' the dishes? (*Black-Eyed Pea breaks out of the vamp step. The music stops.*)
BLACK-EYED PEA
Nope. 'Less I cook, then I do them. I take 'em and break 'em and throw them out the window. Better watch out, puppy, I'll break you! (*She laughs. The music resumes and she returns to the vamp pattern.*) Bubble, do you like grits?
BUBBLE
Never heard of 'em.
BLACK-EYED PEA
You better, honey, if you gonna be my friend. (*Pause. The music stops.*) How 'bout black?
BUBBLE
Well . . . maybe. (*in a tiny voice*) White?

BLACK-EYED PEA
  We'll see.
BLACK-EYED PEA and BUBBLE
  God? (*Thunder. Lights flash. The two children look at one another in astonishment.*)
BLACK-EYED PEA
  Come on, we're gonna get rained on. (*They run out, holding hands.*)

Scene vi   Old Glue Needle and Wet Paint Bill

Bubble and Black-Eyed Pea enter from one side of the stage and collide with Diana Dumbstrut and the Stale Cake Company coming from the other side.

DADDY TUTTI-FRUIT HAT
  Hey, kids, where ya been? We missed you. Where's your recipes for the Goodie Cookie and the Big Magic Cookie Pan Winner Pie? (*to Black-Eyed Pea*) Where's your queen crown, baby?
OREO COOKIE MAN
  What's the matter, honey? Did your mammy call you home?
CAPTAIN STEAL
  (*to Bubble*) Hey, little fella, you need your spaced beamer helmet with the built-in, far out pockets for cheat notes!
STALE CAKE COMPANY
  (*chanting a football yell with Diana Dumbstrut as the cheerleader*) Well! Come! On! Kids! Get! With! It! (*Black-Eyed Pea and Bubble hesitate in silence.*)
BUBBLE
  Well, what do you have?
STALE CAKE COMPANY
  (*chanting*) What! Do! We! Have! (*Theme: "The Stale Cake Com-*

pany." The members of the Stale Cake Company croon the background as Daddy Tutti-Fruit Hat sings.)

DADDY TUTTI-FRUIT HAT

It's a real thing, it's a love thing,
It's a god thing, it's a . . .

BUBBLE

Have you got any flutes or lutes? (*The Stale Cake Company people don't know what he means; they ad-lib and mumble nervously.*)

BLACK-EYED PEA

Any directions for making friends with fishes?

CAPTAIN STEAL

I've got a few ideas about that. (*The others motion for him to say no more.*)

BUBBLE

Do you give lessons in shoemaking? I'd like to make myself a pair of boots. (*Diana Dumbstrut shows her boots. Bubble shakes his head.*)

BLACK-EYED PEA

Do you bake your own bread, Miss Doughie? I'd just love to have a recipe for some of that bread. (*As Black-Eyed Pea turns away, Dorothy Doughie gestures as if to hit Black-Eyed Pea with her spoon but is stopped by the others. The Stale Cake Company is growling, becoming very hostile.*)

BUBBLE

Can you skip stones? (*Members of the Stale Cake Company, outraged, mutter: "Sk . . . sk . . . sk . . ." "What?"*)

BLACK-EYED PEA

Do you have any seeds?

DADDY TUTTI-FRUIT HAT

Aaaaaahhhhh! You mean Super Socko Space Steamin' Silver-Coated One-A-Days . . . (*He pulls a pill bottle out of his coat.*)

BUBBLE

No! Just vegetable seeds. I'd like to have a little garden by my back door . . . Do you have any rutabaga seeds? (*Members of the Stale Cake Company mutter: "Root . . . roo . . . tabay . . ."*

"Cake . . ." "Seed . . ." "Roota . . .") Or maybe celery or carrots if you don't have rutabagas.

BLACK-EYED PEA

You got any directions in that wagon on how to grow black-eyed peas? (*Bubble and Black-Eyed Pea laugh. The members of the Stale Cake Company are bewildered.*) No? Then you take one bag of black dirt and some water, a hoe, one rake, and then seeds and some cow pie. You must have plenty of cow pie around here, Miss Doughie. (*Bubble and Black-Eyed Pea laugh. This infuriates the Stale Cake Company people. They growl and chomp, cartoon fashion.*)

DADDY TUTTI-FRUIT HAT

Hey, I guess we'll have to teach you two a lesson. You kids don't seem to know what's good for you in life. You don't know what you need to live. We'll make you kids rich and fat! Cute and glamorous!

DOROTHY DOUGHIE

Strong and rich!

OREO COOKIE MAN

We'll give you kids linoleum shoes with shiny fingers!

DIANA DUMBSTRUT

Gold jet pants!

CAPTAIN STEAL

Doll sets that swim in the sink!

ELECTRIC PIGGYBANK MAN

A bike with parties inside!

DADDY TUTTI-FRUIT HAT

And fat red candy face electric cow silver eggbeaters! (*As he says this, the members of the Stale Cake Company turn on the two children and begin to chase them in slow motion, brandishing their props as clubs, growling and sneering. As they chase the children, Old Glue Needle and Wet Paint Bill enter with their umbrella-repairing wagon, which they push to the center of the stage. The group comes circling toward them; the two rest calmly against the wagon and the children run past them. The children then sit down, downstage of the two men, and the Stale Cake Company people halt suddenly, staring at the newcomers.*)

WET PAINT BILL

Anybody need their umbrella fixed? Oh, see here, Glue Needle, some folks is out here in the street today. My, my, you all exercise while you runnin' away or are you playin' "tick-a-tag"? . . . "catch-a-baby"? Now that's a fine game.

OLD GLUE NEEDLE

Uh-hmm. (*with a pointed glance at the Electric Piggybank Man*) Do you ever play "pig in the blanket"?

WET PAINT BILL

Or "poke the mule with the umbrella"? (*As the Oreo Cookie Man replies, Dorothy Doughie sings "Swanee" and pantomimes strumming a banjo. The Oreo Cookie Man plays this broadly, an obvious caricature.*)

OREO COOKIE MAN

No, brother. No, we're just out here on the street today, sellin' our recipes, brother. Gimme some skin. Ruby begonia. (*He extends his hand to Wet Paint Bill, who just looks at him.*)

WET PAINT BILL

Uh, what you do, mister? Did you fall into the mud pen?

OREO COOKIE MAN

(*maintaining a fake smile*) Chitlins!

WET PAINT BILL

Look, Glue Needle, he fell into the muddy pen.

OREO COOKIE MAN

Corn pone!

WET PAINT BILL

Why, sir, you got yourself a dirty face.

OREO COOKIE MAN

White Cadillac!

WET PAINT BILL

Here, take my handkerchief and wipe that off! (*He pulls out a handkerchief and wipes the Oreo Cookie Man's face, revealing white skin. The Oreo Cookie Man panics.*)

OREO COOKIE MAN

Oh, no! (*He runs to the Dream Wagon and grabs a whiteface mask. He adopts a Chamber of Commerce manner.*) Very glad to meet you out here on the street today, sir. (*He turns to Daddy Tutti-Fruit Hat and they shake hands.*) All right, George, I'll bring the insurance policy by tomorrow.

DADDY TUTTI-FRUIT HAT

Thanks so much for stopping by, Jim. Say hello to the wife and kids. (*The Oreo Cookie Man steps behind Daddy Tutti-Fruit Hat and removes the mask.*)

WET PAINT BILL

You folks pardon us, we're just out in the street today doin' our work.

OLD GLUE NEEDLE

Some of you seem to be standin' around. I wonder if you have need of our expertise and skill.

WET PAINT BILL

Ten cents takes care of it, work guaranteed against hailstorm and lightning.

OLD GLUE NEEDLE

Unless you deserve it, and then of course you're goin' to get it anyway. (*The sound of thunder is produced on the percussion.*)

WET PAINT BILL

We'd be pleased to help you out.

STALE CAKE COMPANY

(*chanting*) Well! What! Do! You! Do! (*Theme: "Old Glue Needle and Wet Paint Bill." * Old Glue Needle and Wet Paint Bill sing the first part a cappella.*)

OLD GLUE NEEDLE

Umbrellas . . .

WET PAINT BILL

Umbrellas . . .

(*The members of the Stale Cake Company cower around the ladder.*)

*Music on page 170.

OLD GLUE NEEDLE and WET PAINT BILL

>*Umbrellas repaired, parasols mended,*
>*Let us take you back to where the Lord intended.*

(*The orchestra picks up the song. The two men dance a gentle, old-fashioned vaudeville soft-shoe routine.*)

>*He's Old Glue Needle and I'm Wet Paint Bill.*
>*If you need anything mended,*
>*Just ask us and we will*
>*Be glad to do with a stitch and a dab,*
>*But you better let us fix you*
>*Before it gets too bad.*

>*Umbrellas repaired, parasols mended,*
>*Let us get you back to where the Lord intended.*
>*Umbrellas repaired, ten pennies if you will . . .*

OLD GLUE NEEDLE

>*Done by Old Glue Needle . . .*

WET PAINT BILL

>*. . . and Wet Paint Bill.*

(*They sing the melody on "doo" as children enter, bringing umbrellas for repair. The children cross past the Stale Cake Company and out with repaired umbrellas. The members of the Stale Cake Company try to entice them, but the children ignore them.*)

OLD GLUE NEEDLE and WET PAINT BILL

>*If the rain's coming in and you're catching cold,*
>*There's a good medicine, so I been told:*
>*Go down to the meadow*
>*In the full moonlight*
>*And say hello to the Lord—*
>*Now you be polite.*

>*He'll give you your share,*
>*That's as he intended.*
>*So hurry on, mister, get your canvas mended.*
>*Umbrellas repaired, hope our work pleases you,*

But if you wanta get fixed quick
Put on your dancin' shoes.
(*They continue the dance routine, making remarks to each other as they dance.*)

OLD GLUE NEEDLE

How ya doin', Bill?

WET PAINT BILL

Oh, tolerable! (*Old Glue Needle sits on Wet Paint Bill's lap.*)

OLD GLUE NEEDLE

A puppet! I want something now, Mama! . . . Get in the boat, Bill! Lewis and Clark! (*They pretend to row a boat.*)

WET PAINT BILL

Oh, explorers! (*Old Glue Needle stands in front of the Stale Cake Company as Wet Paint Bill poses on one foot, his hand over his eyes as if looking far into the distance. Wet Paint Bill looks toward the audience as Old Glue Needle stares at the Stale Cake Company.*)

OLD GLUE NEEDLE

It's still there, Bill.

WET PAINT BILL

Oh, it is?

OLD GLUE NEEDLE

Why, didn't you think it would be?

WET PAINT BILL

I thought it would be, but I don't think it should be . . . (*They turn and walk upstage with tiny, mincing steps.*)

OLD GLUE NEEDLE

Tiny steps.

WET PAINT BILL

Minuscule. (*They put their umbrellas behind their heads and lean back on them as if against pillows.*)

OLD GLUE NEEDLE

Bedtime. (*He pretends to row a boat; Wet Paint Bill climbs into the boat and helps row.*) Let's go . . . England!

WET PAINT BILL

France!

OLD GLUE NEEDLE
> Germany!

WET PAINT BILL
> All by boat!

OLD GLUE NEEDLE
> Kansas!

OLD GLUE NEEDLE and WET PAINT BILL
> (*singing*)
>> *So remember, my friends,*
>> *We hope you take it to heart,*
>> *When the old world looks confused*
>> *And your mind is comin' apart,*
>> *Take a dab from Old Glue Needle*
>> *And a stitch from Wet Paint Bill,*
>> *Fix the tears in your umbrella,*
>> *Let us paint your windowsill.*
>> *Get the life that's good and simple,*
>> *It's not easy but you try,*
>> *Find a message for your neighbor,*
>> *He will read it by and by . . .*

DADDY TUTTI-FRUIT HAT
> (*writing everything down in a tiny notebook, mumbling to himself*) "He will read it by and by."

OLD GLUE NEEDLE and WET PAINT BILL
> (*singing*)
>> *You'll hurry to the meadow*
>> *Where the water's runnin' still . . .*

WET PAINT BILL
> (*speaking over his shoulder to the Oreo Cookie Man*) If you don't get that face cleaned up, you never goin' to make it! (*The Oreo Cookie Man growls at him.*)

OLD GLUE NEEDLE and WET PAINT BILL
> (*singing*)
>> *Where you'll meet Old Glue Needle*
>> *And Wet Paint Bill.*
> (*By the end of the song they are seated on the repair wagon.*)

DADDY TUTTI-FRUIT HAT

Well, well, that's all well and good, fellas. I mean I digga dig, I dig your spiel, I dig your schtick, but nobody uses umbrellas any more these days . . . We've got everything you kids could possibly want or need. Whatta ya need, huh?

BLACK-EYED PEA

Could you fix my umbrella?

DADDY TUTTI-FRUIT HAT

(*confidently*) Could we fix your umbrella! (*to the Stale Cake Company*) Could we fix her umbrella? (*to Black-Eyed Pea*) Why, sure, honey, give it here . . . (*He grabs her umbrella and the Stale Cake Company huddles, growling and thrashing. Daddy Tutti-Fruit Hat emerges from the huddle with Dorothy Doughie's spoon. He takes it to Black-Eyed Pea.*) A Dorothy Doughie! (*Black-Eyed Pea looks at it in disgust.*)

BLACK-EYED PEA

Could I have my umbrella back?

DADDY TUTTI-FRUIT HAT

Whatta ya mean? Put it over your head . . . (*He swings the spoon over his head, demonstrating.*)

OREO COOKIE MAN

Oh, that's a dandy, that's a dandy! (*Daddy Tutti-Fruit Hat sees that Black-Eyed Pea is not interested, and he strides back to the group. Again they jam together, growling, and Daddy Tutti-Fruit Hat emerges with Diana Dumbstrut's giant eggbeater.*)

DADDY TUTTI-FRUIT HAT

A Diana Dumbstrut '72 model! Chrome reverse wheels, candy apple red . . . put it right over your head and turn it real fast . . . (*He demonstrates.*)

DIANA DUMBSTRUT

It's just like hers! (*Black-Eyed Pea shakes her head. Daddy Tutti-Fruit Hat returns to the group and emerges with Black-Eyed Pea's parasol.*)

DADDY TUTTI-FRUIT HAT

Here! (*He gives the parasol back to her.*)

OLD GLUE NEEDLE

She's got you whipped, Mister Fruit Hat.

DADDY TUTTI-FRUIT HAT

I know what you people need! A little bit of Stale Cake! I want each and every one of you to take one of these individually cellophane-wrapped packages of Stale Cake . . . from Daddy Tutti-Fruit Hat, with love. (*The members of the Stale Cake Company say "Mmmmm!" lick their lips, and pat their tummies. They croon the theme song off-key as Daddy Tutti-Fruit Hat takes pieces of cake wrapped in cellophane from the Dream Wagon and gives them to Wet Paint Bill, Old Glue Needle, and the children. They bite into the cake, but obviously it is no taste treat.*)

OLD GLUE NEEDLE

Well, we're sorry to say this, but . . .

WET PAINT BILL

This cake . . .

BUBBLE

This cake . . .

BLACK-EYED PEA

. . . is stale!

WET PAINT BILL

You should come to our house sometime. We got *good* cake.

OLD GLUE NEEDLE

You could put a cover over it and keep it moist.

BUBBLE

You need a recipe for this stuff?

BLACK-EYED PEA

Pardon me, Miss Doughie, maybe your bowl is a little on the dirty side of things.

DADDY TUTTI-FRUIT HAT

All right! We've got your number, sweetheart! (*The members of the Stale Cake Company glower at the men and the children and exit in a huff.*)

OLD GLUE NEEDLE

We'll see you, Mister Fruit Hat!

WET PAINT BILL

My, my, never tasted the stuff they were passin' out.

OLD GLUE NEEDLE

That's like sellin' vinegar for water 'cause it comes in a bottle.

WET PAINT BILL

(*to Bubble and Black-Eyed Pea*) Say, you want to join us in a song?

BUBBLE and BLACK-EYED PEA

Yeah!

OLD GLUE NEEDLE

OK. One, two, three . . . (*Reprise: "Old Glue Needle and Wet Paint Bill."* They all sing on "doo," pretending to play musical instruments, parading with umbrellas, and marching upstage. Upstage, they turn to sing to the audience.*)

ALL

> *Get the life that's good and simple,*
> *It's not easy but you try,*
> *Find a message for your neighbor,*
> *He will read it by and by . . .*

(*Thunder. They open their umbrellas, holding them like parasols behind them.*)

> *You'll hurry to the meadow*
> *Where the water's runnin' still,*
> *There you'll meet Old Glue Needle*
> *And Wet Paint Bill.*

(*They close their umbrellas and dance out as the lights cross-fade and the Matchbox House slides into place.*)

*Music on page 170.

Scene vii   Mother Mary
and the Matchbox House

Bubble, Black-Eyed Pea, Wet Paint Bill, and Old Glue Needle slide in, greeting Mother Mary and laughing. Mother Mary, seated in an armchair, is painting at an easel.

MOTHER MARY

Hi! I'm just paintin' up this picture of the sun. Ain't this nice? I've been learning how to draw and paint with the kids these days. But I got up this morning and sat out on the step in the yard and painted this picture of the sun sitting in the sky. Don't that make a picture, though? Hurry up, Bill, lemonade needs squeezin' before the cookies get cold. Needle, get the glasses out, if you please. Oh, my! Who's this? Well, guests in the Matchbox! How do you do? (*Bubble and Black-Eyed Pea go to her and sit on the arms of her chair.*)

BUBBLE and BLACK-EYED PEA

Hello, ma'am.

MOTHER MARY

What's your name?

BLACK-EYED PEA

Black-Eyed Pea.

BUBBLE

Bubble.

MOTHER MARY

Well, I'm Mother Mary, the cook. How do you do? Tell me, how did you two get here? Nobody don't come to this place unless they come with Needle and Bill. What you gotta say?

BUBBLE

Bill and Glue Needle helped us from some trouble.

MOTHER MARY

Oh yeah, what's the matter?

128

BLACK-EYED PEA

Well, these people were trying to chase us and stuff.

WET PAINT BILL

Chase ya? They'd like to turn you into butter.

OLD GLUE NEEDLE

They looked to me like they were picking after strawberries.

MOTHER MARY

Well, what were ya doing to get yourself chased around the street on a hot day like this?

BUBBLE

Well, they wanted us to buy something.

MOTHER MARY

Buy what?

BLACK-EYED PEA

Oh, all kinds of stuff nobody needed.

BUBBLE

We didn't need it.

MOTHER MARY

Like what?

BLACK-EYED PEA

Oh, some portable something or other. You're supposed to put it on your head. It's got lights, plays music, and cooks up some toasted waffle or something.

BUBBLE

Yeah, and tells you the time.

BLACK-EYED PEA

Yeah, and glows in the dark.

BUBBLE

Yeah, and smells like pine needles when you squeeze it.

OLD GLUE NEEDLE

And has a heater in it.

WET PAINT BILL

And it can be used as a can opener for sardines, oh my!

MOTHER MARY

Ah me, oh my! Does it take your shoes off, too, and rub your tired old feet? I wonder if it knows how to squeeze lemonade and do the washing! If it can, I just might get myself a couple of them things and tell these old two to get on. (*She laughs*.) But what you two do to get them sellin' folks to chase you around the place?

BUBBLE

Nothing. Just asked them if they knew how to skip stones.

MOTHER MARY

What'd they say?

BUBBLE

No.

BLACK-EYED PEA

Uh-huh.

MOTHER MARY

What else?

BLACK-EYED PEA

Oh, and if they could bake bread.

MOTHER MARY

What'd they say?

BUBBLE

No.

BLACK-EYED PEA

And if they had black-eyed pea seeds.

MOTHER MARY

What'd they say?

BUBBLE and BLACK-EYED PEA

No!

MOTHER MARY

(*turning to Wet Paint Bill and Old Glue Needle*) And what'd you two say?

WET PAINT BILL

Oh, nothin'!

OLD GLUE NEEDLE

Just asked them if they could mend an umbrella.

MOTHER MARY

Oh, oh.

BUBBLE and BLACK-EYED PEA

And they said no.

MOTHER MARY
Oh! What kind of people can't even patch up an old umbrella?

WET PAINT BILL
Most kinds, I expect, these days. Most folks just throw away everything that's gettin' the least bit old and buy something new.

OLD GLUE NEEDLE
They don't fix nothin', Mary.

WET PAINT BILL
They don't care to preserve nothin' old, nothin' that's been good to them for years. Instead they're looking for something new.

OLD GLUE NEEDLE
And shiny. New and shiny. Well, I saw an umbrella the other day that didn't even look like one. The only way I could tell the fella thought that's what it was, was it started to rain and he stuck the damn thing over his head. I'll show you what it looked like. (*He goes to the easel and begins to paint a picture of the umbrella.*) It had a window here and another one here and a third window here, and it had a fourth window right here in the center. Looked more like a decorated rocket ship with windows to me. Been better off with a garbage can cover.

WET PAINT BILL
I'd have to make up something to do with most of the stuff they had to sell. Why, they had one thing they called a ramma-stramma . . .

OLD GLUE NEEDLE
Here, now, watch your language in front of the kids. Mary, it seems to me that most folks today ain't even heard of a glass of plain water.

WET PAINT BILL
They looked like they'd never heard of plain old people.

BUBBLE
There wasn't one thing they had that I wanted.

BLACK-EYED PEA
Me neither.

MOTHER MARY
Why, what did those folks go by? What name?

BUBBLE

> The Stale Cake Company. (*They laugh.*)

MOTHER MARY

> Well, now that figures. There ain't nothin' to do with a hunk of stale cake, 'cept nothin'.

BUBBLE

> Yeah, but they were giving away lots of pieces of that cake, and all the kids were taking it and cheering and shouting "Wa-hoo!" and puttin' it in their shopping bags.

BLACK-EYED PEA

> Yeah, and paying Big Money for all their stuff.

BUBBLE

> Some of them got some really shiny stuff to take home. Maybe we should try it.

BLACK-EYED PEA

> Don't you say it. You want to turn into a pig or somethin', boy?

WET PAINT BILL

> They had this one man — looked just like a pig.

OLD GLUE NEEDLE

> They had this one *pig* that looked just like a *man*.

WET PAINT BILL

> Oink, oink . . . Here's the lemonade and here's the cookies. Hot and fresh. (*Wet Paint Bill and Old Glue Needle make a production out of serving the food. They sing a fanfare, "ta-tata-ta-tata," and march to the children and Mary, carrying the food and singing.*)

WET PAINT BILL and OLD GLUE NEEDLE

> *Oh, the Stale Cake*
> *Is the real cake!*

WET PAINT BILL

> That's just how the Stale Cake song went. OK, now. Everybody take one of these. You're gonna get a chance now to try a special old recipe of mine. A long time ago this was given to me by my mother. She said to me, "Bill, one of these days, you're gonna be on your own and you're gonna get a chance to make this yourself.

Then you can give it to somebody and have them taste it." This is
old, Mother Mary, now tell me what it's like.

MOTHER MARY

Well, Bill, it tastes old (*they laugh*) . . . but it's delicious.

BUBBLE

Wow! These are the best cookies I ever tasted!

BLACK-EYED PEA

Uh-huh!

MOTHER MARY

You think so? Tell 'em, you two.

OLD GLUE NEEDLE

Well, you see, not everybody thinks these here cookies are the best
they've ever tasted.

BUBBLE

Why? They're terrific.

BLACK-EYED PEA

Really!

WET PAINT BILL

That's right. But not everybody likes the same things.

OLD GLUE NEEDLE

Now, you know and I know Mother Mary's cookies are the best.

WET PAINT BILL

I know so many people that think that other cookies are better.

OLD GLUE NEEDLE

Just like those people that were eating away on that stale
cake.

WET PAINT BILL

And if you don't know what's good in the first place, how you
gonna tell the difference when you see it?

MOTHER MARY, OLD GLUE NEEDLE, and WET PAINT BILL

When it's lookin' ya in the face.

MOTHER MARY

No sir, you gotta know to taste my sugar and spice. And that ain't
easy for some folks. Now, you two, you like to sit up in a tree?
And you, out on the roof?

BLACK-EYED PEA and BUBBLE
> Yeah.

MOTHER MARY
> Fresh water?

BLACK-EYED PEA
> Yeah.

MOTHER MARY
> And the wind and singing?

BLACK-EYED PEA and BUBBLE
> Yeah.

MOTHER MARY
> And quiet times in the back patch?

BLACK-EYED PEA and BUBBLE
> Yeah.

MOTHER MARY
> So maybe your old nose is just in fine shape to taste a cookie and
> know it's settin' fine. But don't you think, babies, that everybody
> sees it, 'cause there's plenty of people out there wantin' a portable
> whatever-it-is, just to make them feel happy. Amen to that.

ALL
> Amen.

MOTHER MARY
> But anyway, we know what we like and we're doing it. Ain't we?
> Let's enjoy it.

ALL
> Yeah! (*They applaud and ad-lib as they eat and drink during
> Winde's entrance. Winde is dressed as a grocery store worker, and
> he carries a bag of groceries.*)

WINDE
> Groceries!

MOTHER MARY
> OK, honey, put 'em back there anywhere. Thank you. (*Old Glue
> Needle brings out an ironing board covered with a lace cloth; a
> piano keyboard rests on the board. He puts it in front of Mother
> Mary.*) Here's one of my favorite things. Bubble, Black-Eyed Pea,
> come over here. Bill and Needle, come over here and gather

round. I never did find room for a piano in here 'cause it's so small here in this Matchbox. But I got Needle to pull this here old keyboard in here. Now I'm just fine. It's kind of magic. I just push on the keys and out comes the music. (*She "plays" on the keyboard, and a piano is heard playing "Sweet Jesus, Precious Savior."**)

BUBBLE

I don't hear it.

MOTHER MARY

That's what I mean, baby. That's like the cookie: Ya can't taste it 'til ya taste it, and with this old thing ya can't hear it 'til ya hear it. But when you do hear it, honey, you HEAR it! And we're hearin' it just fine. Right, you two?

WET PAINT BILL and OLD GLUE NEEDLE

Right! (*Mother Mary plays on the keyboard again, and a few more measures of the song are heard.*)

BUBBLE

Let me try!

MOTHER MARY

OK. Come on. (*Bubble sits at the keyboard and tries to play, but nothing happens.*)

BUBBLE

I just don't hear it.

MOTHER MARY

Try it now, right there. (*She takes Bubble's finger and places it on the keyboard. As she does so, each of the men places a hand on one of Bubble's shoulders. This time a few measures of the song are heard.*)

BUBBLE

Wow! It works!

MOTHER MARY

Of course.

OLD GLUE NEEDLE

Really!

*Music on page 168.

WET PAINT BILL

Don't say. (*Mother Mary, Black-Eyed Pea, and the cast sing "Sweet Jesus, Precious Savior."*)

MOTHER MARY

> *Lead me home,*
> *Lead me home, now,*
> *Sweet, sweet Jesus!*
> *O-o-oh!*

(*The members of the cast take positions at the back of the auditorium, in the balcony, and in the wings to sing "oooh!" as an accompaniment to the solo lines.*)

> *Through the storm,*
> *Through the night,*
> *Lead me home!*

BLACK-EYED PEA

> *I am tired,*
> *I am weary,*
> *And the world grows*
> *Cold around me.*
> *Precious Jesus,*
> *Precious Savior,*
> *Lead me home!*

BLACK-EYED PEA	CAST
Lead me home . . .	*Lead me home now!*
Lead me home . . .	*Lead me home now!*
Lead me home . . .	*Lead me home now!*
Lead me home through	
the night . . .	*Lead me home . . .*
Through the storm . . .	*Lead me home!*
Lead me home!	

ALL

> *Oh Lord, lead me home!*

BLACK-EYED PEA	CAST
I am tired . . .	*Lead me home!*
I am weary . . .	*Lead me home!*
And the world grows . . .	*Lead me home!*
Cold around me . . .	*Lead me home!*

ALL

> *Precious Jesus*
> *Precious Savior,*
> *Lead me home!*

(*Black-Eyed Pea and Bubble run out, waving and saying good-bye to Mother Mary, Winde, Wet Paint Bill, and Old Glue Needle, who remain at the keyboard singing. The lights fade down. The Matchbox House slides offstage.*)

Scene viii   "Get, Get, Get!"

Winde addresses the audience from a pool of light.

WINDE

Very nice. There's a real nice breeze blowin' through that Matchbox House . . . Just what a body needs to feel right — a little nudge from the spirit on a warm day . . . but on the other hand, I feel the wind coming down the other direction with just more than a little smell of something rotten in it. Smells to me like a piece of stale cake. I don't believe that everybody that bought a recipe today was exactly filled with smiles for his fellow man. You know how it is — when somebody gets something new that's his alone and his only, he doesn't want to share it with his neighbor . . . Yup, I think I detect the smell of burnt cake drifting by my nose . . . What do you think? (*Boogie lead-in to "Get, Get, Get!" Ricky and Ronn stride in from the right and left wings and hostilely confront each other. Winde exits.*)

RONN

Oh!

RICKY

Yeah!

RONN

No!

RICKY
    Huh!
RONN
    Huh!
RICKY
    Huh! (*Black-Eyed Pea and Bubble enter and greet the two boys.*)
BUBBLE
    Hi!
RONN
    Get out of here! (*Black-Eyed Pea and Bubble run out.*)
RICKY
    Go on! Mine is!
RONN
    No! Mine is!
RICKY
    We'll see, we'll see!
RONN
    We'll see nothin'!
RICKY
    See this! (*He punches Ronn in the eye. Theme: "The Stale Cake Company," march tempo. Dorothy Doughie enters, sees the conflict, and blows her whistle for the Electric Piggybank Man and the Dream Wagon to enter.*)
DOROTHY DOUGHIE
    (*sweetly*) What's the matter, boys? Did you have an argument?
RONN
    The recipe I bought from the Stale Cake is best! And I'll prove it!
DOROTHY DOUGHIE
    (*again sweetly*) Oohhh! You're right! Well then, here. (*speaking in a gang moll's aside to Ronn*) Buy now, pay later! (*She gets a wooden saber from the Dream Wagon and hands it to Ronn, hiding it from Ricky.*)
RICKY
    No, no, no! Mine's the best and I'll prove it!
DOROTHY DOUGHIE
    (*sweetly*) Oohhh! I'm sure it is. (*speaking again as a gang moll,*

this time to Ricky) Today, for you, a discount. (*She gives him a saber also, hiding it from Ronn. She sings to the tune of "Good Ship Lollipop."*)

> *On the good ship* Kill a Lot . . .

(*She giggles and runs off with the Electric Piggybank Man and the Dream Wagon. Ronn and Ricky begin to fight. Sheila and Maureen push between them to the center of the stage.*)

SHEILA

(*chanting as she reads from a recipe*) Take two cups of lever and two cups of jever. Wait 'til it's hard and it's good forever!

MAUREEN

Oh yeah! That's nothin'! Wait until you see the size of mine. Besides, mine has an elevator in it! (*A guitar makes a musical comment. Maureen speaks to the guitarist.*) Hey! That's pretty good, man.

SHEILA

Oh yeah!

MAUREEN

Yeah! And when I'm the head one, you're goin' to be the end one!

RICKY

Same for you, too! (*A battle ensues with Ronn fighting Ricky and Sheila fighting Maureen. Captain Steal enters.*)

CAPTAIN STEAL

Aye, maties! Aye, maties! Only ladies and gents! Please! Here, try one of these!

CHILDREN

Wow! Far out!

CAPTAIN STEAL

This is the Super Ding-A-Ling Buzz Ball! (*He pulls out a grenade device.*) Spreads all sorts of disease! (*chanting*) With one of these, you can smash in their heads! Get one of these, you can knock them all dead.

CHILDREN

I'll take one of those! I'll take ten of those, from you! Where's mine?

ELECTRIC PIGGYBANK MAN

Good kids! That's only $14.92!

CAPTAIN STEAL

Here, try a case! (*The battle resumes. The members of the Stale Cake Company weave among the children, yelling and selling weapons. Underscore: lead-in to "Get, Get, Get!"*)

ELECTRIC PIGGYBANK MAN

Weapons for war! Weapons for war! Programs for the war!

CLINTON

(*chanting*) Now everybody, I mean everybody, just listen to me! 'Cause, baby, I plan on takin' over with my recipe. So everybody just cool back and settle down, 'cause I'm takin' over in this town!

ARTIE and CYN

(*taking turns chanting phrases*) One cup of flabbers, one cup of gebats. Man, when we get done with this, it's going to be bad! Right on!

CLINTON

Bad! You mean sad!

BRIDGET

Yours stinks!

ARTIE

You're finks!

CYN

(*chanting*) This is a Dobas Franges Fretter, and there can be nothing better, and if you guys don't believe us, you'd better leave us! (*Some of the children throw grenades at others. Another fight begins.*)

KIM

(*singing*) The Stale Cake is the real cake! (*chanting*) And I'm the one that's going to do the big bake that's going to break me into the lead! Here's all I need! Can you believe it? Well, you can see it! And pretty soon, you're all goin' to eat it!

OREO COOKIE MAN

Right on, soul sister! You heard it from Mr. Oreo! (*All perform a minstrel routine of hand-clapping and seat-slapping as "Swanee" is played on the piano, underscoring the Oreo Cookie Man's*

speech. He begins to chant.) Hello, I see you're on the go. But
you've gotta have your flapper gun, you know! Here's your
crown, go to town, just waitin' for you to gun 'em down! (*Kim
starts to take a toy bazooka from him.*) That'll be $6.97, honey!
(*She pays him with Big Money and then pretends to shoot
everyone with the gun. A percussion instrument sounds the
shots.*)

STEVEN

(*chanting in rhythm with the music*) Keeno! Neato! I repeato! I
just won the championship with my recipe for a sailing ship! I'll
take the lead 'cause I got the speed to do the deed! You guys are
creeps! Yes, I repeat, you guys are creeps! Your stuff is cheap!
(*speaking conversationally*) Why don't you take a leap into a dirty
dish pan! I am the man! (*All attack Steven. Diana Dumbstrut
leads the Stale Cake Company and the children in a yell.*)

ALL

Fight, fight, fight! Kill, kill, kill! Fight, fight, fight, fight, you're a
pill! Yay! War! (*All fight and dance. Jenny enters with a
megaphone. They all chant.*) Mine's the best, mine's the best,
everybody knows that mine's the best!

DEBBIE

(*chanting*) Fiddy biddy bye, fiddy biddy bo, you're a little too
smart so you've got to go! (*She knocks Jenny to the ground.*)

ALL

Yay! (*The following lines are chanted.*)

DIANA DUMBSTRUT

So take your own!

CAPTAIN STEAL

Take it home!

DOROTHY DOUGHIE

But you've gotta make sure that you're all alone!

OREO COOKIE MAN

Don't let anybody touch it, remember that!

ELECTRIC PIGGYBANK MAN

Keep all the good stuff under your hat!

DADDY TUTTI-FRUIT HAT

Remember . . . Stale Cake, Stale Cake, S-T-A-L-E . . . Stale Cake!

ALL

(*repeating about six times*) Stale Cake! Stale Cake! Stale Cake! Stale Cake! Stale Cake! Stale Cake! (*Piano theme: "Sweet Jesus, Precious Savior." Black-Eyed Pea and Bubble enter with lemonade and cookies for all.*)

BLACK-EYED PEA

Hi, you guys, want some lemonade? It's fresh and just squeezed and made of fresh real lemons.

BUBBLE

And fresh cookies, too, still hot.

RONN

Gimme one of those cookies. I'll pay five. How much are they?

MAUREEN

I'll take a dozen. I've got plenty of money. And put it on my elevator.

AUDREY

Give me some lemonade.

ARTIE

Don't give her nothin'. She ain't got no money. I got most of it.

SHEILA

Give me lots of those cookies, I've got Big Money. (*A melee erupts with everyone yelling and grabbing.*)

BLACK-EYED PEA

You don't need money, we've got plenty. They're free.

BUBBLE

Yes. See?

CAPTAIN STEAL

You don't give nothin' away!

ELECTRIC PIGGYBANK MAN

If you got somethin' somebody wants, you make 'em pay.

DIANA DUMBSTRUT

(*leading them in a cheer*) Say "pay"!

ALL
  Pay!
DIANA DUMBSTRUT
  Say "yay"!
ALL
  Yay!
BLACK-EYED PEA
  Why pay when everything's free . . .
BUBBLE
  And good . . .
BLACK-EYED PEA
  Today! (*Theme: "Get, Get, Get!"* * *Daddy Tutti-Fruit Hat whips
  everyone but Bubble and Black-Eyed Pea into place.*)
DADDY TUTTI-FRUIT HAT
  (*speaking in rhythm*) We won't be underbid, my friends, so listen
  to our story. The best buy in a recipe will make you . . .
DIANA DUMBSTRUT and WOMEN
  (*singing*)
    . . . rich before you're forty!
DADDY TUTTI-FRUIT HAT
  And now, here to tell you more is Captain Steal! (*The girls squeal.
  Ginni crawls to Captain Steal and hugs his leg.*)
GINNI
  I love you, Captain Steal!
CAPTAIN STEAL
  I love you, too, Cookie. (*He recites the verse in rhythm. The cast
  sings "bum-bum" in tempo in the background.*)
    So assemble all your stuff, my friends,
    Your bricks, your gold, and your booty,
    And be sure and buy our recipes
    'Cause if you don't, you will be sorry!
ALL
  (*singing*)
    Ya gotta get, get, get!
    Ya gotta get, get, get!

*Music on page 171.

> *If the world's in trouble*
> *And you don't know what to do,*
> *Ya gotta get, get, get!*
> *Hey hey, hey ho!*
> *Hey hey, hey ho!*

DADDY TUTTI-FRUIT HAT

Now, here comes the Oreo Cookie Man! (*The cast continues to sing "hey hey, hey ho" under the Oreo Cookie Man's speech.*)

OREO COOKIE MAN

Brothers and sisters, brothers and sisters, yeah, yeah, yeah, yeah! (*He recites in rhythm.*)

> *Come here to me!*
> *Come here to me!*
> *Come look me in the eye.*
> *I'll make you rich,*
> *I'll make you happy,*
> *If you'll only let me try!*

(*He leaps back into the group; they sing "bum-bum" in the background as Daddy Tutti-Fruit Hat comes forward again.*)

DADDY TUTTI-FRUIT HAT

And now, Miss Diana Dumbstrut, the Girl with the Golden Goose! Tell 'em, Diana! (*Diana Dumbstrut struts to him.*)

DIANA DUMBSTRUT

First you need a suit! And some shiny boots! And a diamond cookie cutter! (*She blows her whistle and does a backbend. Then she marches in place furiously as the music bursts briefly into a Sousa march and everyone cheers. Then the group resumes the "bum-bum" background.*)

DADDY TUTTI-FRUIT HAT

And now, for the first time in public, the Stale Cake Company's very own Franges Dober Flutter! Only $11.95 at toy department stores everywhere . . . (*speaking rapidly through "included"*) requires-seven-Eveready- Triple- A- Penlight-batteries-batteries-not-included . . . Because I am Daddy Tutti-Fruit Hat and I stand behind each and every one of my Stale Cake Company products, I'm going to be the first to try on the Franges Dober

Flutter. (*He has been putting the gadget on his head as he speaks.*)
Go ahead! (*to one of the crowd*) Turn that thing! (*Everyone
shrieks. The lights go down and the Franges Dober Flutter lights
up. Daddy Tutti-Fruit Hat does a frantic shimmy dance, jumping
up and down in the darkness with the glowing Franges Dober
Flutter on his head. It vaguely resembles a modernistic lamp with
filaments that "spray" out from the base. A burst of music
accompanies this brief display. The Franges Dober Flutter
music ends and the vamp resumes.*) A little bit much for Daddy
Tutti-Fruit Hat! (*He gives the Franges Dober Flutter to the
Electric Piggybank Man and retrieves the Fruit Hat.*) And now
here she is, the world's favorite cream puff, Miss Dorothy
Doughie!

DOROTHY DOUGHIE
> (*singing and dancing in place*)
>> You need a pile of flops
>> And a box of drops
>> And a luster-crusted fretter
>> And a golden chain of Stink-o-Lets . . .
> (*The members of the cast bounce and sway from side to side as
> they sing the following lyrics.*)

ALI
>> *Who-o-o!*

MEN
>> *Nothing could be better!*

ALL
>> *Ya gotta get, get, get!*
>> *Ya gotta get, get, get!*

WOMEN
>> *Oh, you'll never be happy . . .*

MEN
>> *. . . get rich very quick*
>> *Unless you get, get, get!*

DADDY TUTTI-FRUIT HAT
> Now here comes . . . (*the girls squeal*) Captain Steal! (*Ginni
> runs to Captain Steal and clings to his leg.*) What's that,
> sweetheart?

GINNI

> I love Captain Steal!

DADDY TUTTI-FRUIT HAT

> Far out! How old are you, darling?

GINNI

> Seven.

DADDY TUTTI-FRUIT HAT

> Seven. How old are you, Captain Steal? (*Captain Steal lowers his sunglasses and leers.*)

CAPTAIN STEAL

> Uh . . . thirteen! (*Squeals. The crowd sings "gotta get, gotta get, gotta get, get" as background for Captain Steal's lines. He recites in rhythm.*)
>> So step aside, little lady . . .
> (*He kicks Ginni away.*)
>> And witness this.
>> It's a miracle of invention . . .
> (*He shows a gadget resembling a toothbrush with coils and wires.*)
>> For to make you the queen
>> With the streamlined gleam
>> Is this machine's
>> Intention!
> (*He steps aside.*)

DADDY TUTTI-FRUIT HAT

> (*in rhythm*) Try . . . that . . . machine. Now here comes a Stale Cake Company duet!

DIANA DUMBSTRUT and ELECTRIC PIGGYBANK MAN

> (*singing*)
>> *Be sure to do your homework,*
>> *Check your list of don'ts and do's . . .*

ALL

>> Who-o-o!
> (*The crowd resumes the "gotta get" background. Through the rest of this scene there is no recitation; everything is sung.*)

DADDY TUTTI-FRUIT HAT

>> *When you get through*

With our products,
You'll be the Girl
With the Golden Goose!

ALL

Ya gotta get, get, get!
Ya gotta get, get, get!
You'll never be the Train
With the Silver Caboose
Unless you get, get, get!
Buy, buy, assemble or you die!
Yes, get, get, get!

(*The dance begins in earnest. Ideally, the very walls would dance, spoons and chairs would sway, chandeliers would bob. All objects would become animate, swelling, bobbing, and dancing as if borrowed from a Betty Boop cartoon. Various colors of light bathe the dancers, who perform in the style of the gaudiest television spectaculars.*)

BASS VOICES

Get, get, get, get! Ya gotta get, get, get, get!
Ya gotta get, get, get, get! Ya gotta get, get, get!

(*The bass voices continue to sing as the altos join them.*)

ALTO VOICES

Hey hey, hey ho! Hey hey, hey ho!

(*A whistle is blown. The tenors join the altos.*)

TENOR VOICES

Gotta get, gotta get, gotta get, get!
Gotta get, gotta get, gotta get, get!
Gotta get, gotta get, gotta get, get!
Gotta get, gotta get, gotta get, get!

(*A dance sequence with no lyrics begins and lasts for several minutes. The entire cast takes part in the dance. Shifting colored floodlights illuminate the stage and contribute to the motion and activity of the dance. As the dance sequence ends, the cast resumes the lyrics. Dorothy Doughie dances and sings a solo pseudo-jazz counterpoint to the music at a point indicated in the score.*)

ALL	DOROTHY DOUGHIE
Get, get, get, get!	*Shi-poopie tittie*
	ah-doo-da-pow!
Everybody's got to get!	*Chuck-full of moo-moo*
Everybody's got to, got to	*And a poo-poo cow!*
Get, get, get!	*Noodle oodle doodle,*
	Sock-a-whammie doll,
	Money, money,
	and a checkbook!

WOMEN

Got to, got to, got to, got to . . .

MEN

Get, get, get, get, get, get, get!

SOPRANO VOICES	ALTO VOICES
Gotta get . . .	*Got to . . .*
Gotta get . . .	*Got to . . .*
Gotta get . . .	*Got to . . .*
Gotta get!	*Got to!*

ALL

Get, get, get!

(*As the song continues, Dorothy Doughie sings and dances the counterpoint as the others sing and dance to the refrain. The effect is that of barely controlled chaos. Dorothy Doughie finishes in time to sing the final "get, get, get" with the others.*)

ALL	DOROTHY DOUGHIE
Get, get, get, get!	*Shi-pop-a-tutti-fruiti*
Everybody's got to get!	*Poodle and pie!*
Everybody's got to get!	*Hi-floogle-boogie-woogie*
Ya gotta get!	*Pudding cup!*
Ya gotta get!	
Ya gotta g-e-t!	
Get, get, get, get, get!	

(*Smoke fills the stage. People are grabbing, chattering, and arguing. They scurry offstage. Daddy Tutti-Fruit Hat stands at the center, gleefully counting the Big Money. He whoops and runs off.*)

Scene ix   Famine

Winde steps through the smoke dressed as a fireman with yellow boots.

WINDE

Hmmm. Things seem to be getting a little hot around here. A bit smoky. A person could get burned. I got my yellow boots with the buckles, though, in case the floods come, too. Well, my friends, do you know what it's like to think that your house is the only little house on the block, that your new bike is the fastest, or your Dad's the smartest? Well now, if your little house catches on fire and your smartest Dad is trapped inside, and you're on your new red fastest bike just comin' home and you see it burning, you might have a hard time putting out the blaze without the help of a friend or two. I wonder if that ingredient is in your recipe. Add one cup of friends and blend thoroughly into a smooth mixture. Taste for sweetness. Let's look at a few recipes and see how folks are doin'. I'll watch and keep a record. You keep score. (*Winde sits on the rim of the bowl-world, where he is joined by Black-Eyed Pea, Wet Paint Bill, Old Glue Needle, and Bubble. Mother Mary leans against the proscenium. They observe the famine. Barry, Ricky, Steven, Holly, Bridget, and Artie bring out their recipes and gadgets. The children are scattered about the stage, each in his or her own world. All onstage speak and act at once. None of the recipes or devices work. The young people become increasingly frustrated, disgusted, and angry. A voiceover from an offstage microphone reverberates through the first part of the scene; the lines tumble upon one another and often are spoken simultaneously.*)

VOICEOVER

I'll be the King of TV! Get your Stale Cake Company King! Where's your queen crown, baby? Gotta get a king crown, gotta get a king-king, gotta get a king crown! A forty-piece orchestra,

149

your very own forty-piece orchestra, playing "Pomp and Circumstance." (*Falsetto voices hum "Pomp and Circumstance."*) Jupiter and Mars! Venus, Pluto! Be the first kid on your block to get to Jupiter! Stale Cake Company Space Kit! (*The voiceover continues with similar lines from other points in the play. The following speeches and actions overlap one another. Chaos.*)

RICKY

I'll be the King! I'm the TV star! Me and my forty-piece band! When I'm the head one, you'll be the end one . . . maybe you'll be no one! Shuffle to the TV star! (*He kicks his machine and it falls apart.*) It does not work!

HOLLY

What's wrong, it doesn't work!

BRIDGET

Give me that! You've probably got mine.

HOLLY

Yours is probably mine! (*They try out their gadgets and nothing works.*)

HOLLY and BRIDGET

These are wrong! They don't work!

BARRY

Wing-a-ding-ding! Just add one little thing! I am the King! I am the King! (*He pantomimes putting on the King's clothes and gets on his carpet.*) Where's the cheering? Where are the people? Where's the coach? (*He adjusts his crown and tries again.*) My subjects . . . where are the subjects? Where's the Queen? I am the King! I am the King! I'm not the King.

STEVEN

I'll get to the moon! I'll get to Mars! Jupiter, here I come! Take off! Take off! I'm not taking off! I'm not going anywhere! I'm not taking off!

ARTIE

I'll be the star of the Ballet Cookie! Ballet Cookie of a Batch! Tie on my little tutu! Russia, here I come! (*She puts on a tutu and tries a ballet step. Parts of her costume fall off.*) I'm falling apart! It doesn't work! I'm not the star of the Ballet Cookie! (*The voiceover fades out. The children pick up their gadgets and devices and exit in tears as others move onto the stage. Theme: "Don't Be Grabbin' for More Than You've Got." Winde and his group begin to clap the rhythm of the song. The lights are dim. A hole near the floor is backlighted red, and the stage is smoky. The famine sequence is choreographed — people are struggling and stealing, weak with hunger: some are being pulled into the "hell hole." The clapping continues throughout the scene, and the Matchbox House group sings.)*

WINDE

And the land was barren
And nobody's recipe worked;
People were at each other's throats,
And all of the land went berserk.

WINDE, BLACK-EYED PEA, MOTHER MARY, and WET PAINT BILL

Don't be grabbin' for more than you've got,
Just know that you've got what you need.
Don't be grabbin' for more than you've got,
Just know that you've got what you need!

MOTHER MARY

Folks were starvin'!

BLACK-EYED PEA

Nobody knows what to do now!

WINDE

Life's a sad state.

WINDE, BLACK-EYED PEA, MOTHER MARY, and WET PAINT BILL

Taking from your neighbor
And your good friends, too.

ALL

Don't be grabbin' for more than you've got,
Just know that you've got what you need!
Don't be grabbin' for more than you've got,
Just know that you've got what you need!

WINDE

Then the rains came
And the thunder broke.

MOTHER MARY
> *And the Lord sent a wind through the land.*

MOTHER MARY and WET PAINT BILL
> *All the recipes for livin'*
> *Blew away to heaven . . .*

WINDE, BLACK-EYED PEA, MOTHER MARY, and WET PAINT BILL
> *. . . and the people had nowhere to turn.*

> *Don't be grabbin' for more than you've got,*
> *Just know that you've got what you need!*
> *Don't be grabbin' for more than you've got,*
> *Just know that you've got what you need!*

(*The chorus is repeated several times. Daddy Tutti-Fruit Hat appears as a silhouette in a shaft of smoky light, holding a bundle of money high while cracking his whip. He shouts "Money!" and the orchestra shouts back "Devil!" on the beats. Shouting, singing, and percussion build to a frenzy, then fade out as the lights go out. Winde continues to sing the chorus a cappella and changes into his "reporter" coat and hat as the Matchbox House is brought onstage in the darkness.*)

Scene x   State of
the Cookie Land Report

Winde is dressed as a newspaper reporter and carries a note pad and a pen. The Matchbox House is on the stage. Mother Mary, Wet Paint Bill, and Old Glue Needle sit in the Matchbox House listening to Winde.

WINDE
> Well, here I am, pickin' up the pieces, so to speak. State of the Cookie Land Report: The people of Cookie Land are on the

lookout for the Stale Cake Company, which was reported trying to leave town. It seems the people all purchased recipes for the Great Life, for which they paid all their Big Money. And it also seems that none of the recipes worked. And if the recipes did work, the people lost the directions on how to use them. Folks hereabout are very upset and are on the lookout for a sign or two. Meanwhile, the Stale Cake Company waits for the train to leave town. Bubble and Black-Eyed Pea left for Mother Mary's Matchbox. What to do? . . . Well . . . I'm just doing the reporting, not the fixing . . . It's a job for somebody . . . Well, maybe I will leave a small recipe. (*He smiles to himself and mumbles as he writes on his note pad.*) Let's see . . . toss some cake . . . (*He pins the note to the match that props up the rim of the bowl-world.*) See ya later, Bill!

WET PAINT BILL

Mmm-hmmm. (*He waves good-bye as Winde exits.*)

Scene xi   Mother Mary's Advice

Bubble and Black-Eyed Pea enter the Matchbox House on the slide, excited, their words tumbling out.

BUBBLE

Mother Mary, Mother Mary, things are terrible!

BLACK-EYED PEA

Yep. People are never goin' to make it. Everybody's all confused.

BUBBLE

Yeah! We don't know what to do!

BLACK-EYED PEA

What're we goin' to do?

MOTHER MARY

Well, I'm not goin' to say too much on the subject, kids, but if the old lady forgot the recipe, or how to get things together, she should take a lesson from what she sees.

BLACK-EYED PEA

What do you mean? (*Lead-in to "Put It All Together into One Big Bowl!"**)

MOTHER MARY

(*singing*)

> *Now you remember the words of a wise old bird;*
> *Oh, listen to the wisdom of a green bullfrog;*
> *Pay attention to the worms who stay up late at night;*
> *Put your ear down close to a log . . . you will always find*
> *   that . . .*

> *The bird in flight seeks other wings;*
> *The frog wants more singers on the lily pad.*
> *The little old worm likes company, oh yeah,*
> *Just look into a fisherman's can!*

(*speaking*) You won't find just one worm there. No, lots of worms. Supposin' the ants are fixin' to build a pyramid . . . Do you think they'd attempt it divided . . . ? No! (*She continues to sing.*)

> *So if it's raining and cold, with holes in your shoes,*
> *No marmalade, no pennies, no rent!*

(*speaking*) And that's bad because they just come on out with the broom and sweep that homely sawdust lady out the door, you know? Uh-huh . . . (*She continues to sing.*)

> *If there's ice on your nose and the wind blows froze*
> *Down your shirt, putting ice cubes down your back;*
> *If the worst comes to worst and you're ready to turn*
> *Into a stone from the bottom of some deep dark well . . .*

(*speaking*) Well, remember the bird . . . the frog and the worm . . . What they *did*! And just think of the ant — almost forgot the little old ant . . . Just throw open your front door, even if it's winter, and call everybody into your home. Come on in, hurry now! Come now, woo hoo, hurry up, yoo hoo, get on in

*Music on pages 172 and 173.

here! And say . . . We're gonna put it all together in one big bowl! (*She continues to sing.*)

> *Oh, put it all together into one big bowl;*
> *Mix a new batch of cookies, now you've been told!*
> *You'll never be hungry . . . in one big bowl;*
> *Put it all together into one big bowl!*

(*speaking*) Now get on and do the invitin'. Tell 'em all, "Come on in here, 'cause we're gonna put it all together in one big bowl!" OK, hurry up now, invite 'em all in! (*The kids run out waving and calling "'Bye!" Wet Paint Bill and Old Glue Needle placidly strike the set as Mother Mary strolls out.*)

Scene xii   The Message

Black-Eyed Pea and Bubble wander across the stage disconsolately.

BLACK-EYED PEA
   Have you thought of it?
BUBBLE
   Huh-uuh! Did you?
BLACK-EYED PEA
   No.
BUBBLE
   Are you going to give up?
BLACK-EYED PEA
   I don't know. Maybe. (*They think and lean on the match supporting the rim of the bowl-world. They do not see Winde's message.*) She said, "Put it all together in one big bowl," right?
BUBBLE
   Yeah, but what was that about the bird and the ant?
BLACK-EYED PEA
   (*musing*) Put it all together . . . into one big bowl.

BUBBLE

    (*seeing Winde's message*) Hey, what is this? A note . . . (*They read the message.*)

BLACK-EYED PEA

    It says, "Toss some cake . . ."

BUBBLE

    ". . . and drop some money . . ."

BLACK-EYED PEA

    ". . . If you stir just right . . ."

BUBBLE

    ". . . things should turn into honey." (*They read the message again.*)

BLACK-EYED PEA

    Toss some cake, toss some cake . . .

BLACK-EYED PEA and BUBBLE

    Stale cake!

BUBBLE

    Money?

BLACK-EYED PEA

    Big Money!

BLACK-EYED PEA and BUBBLE

    Let's go! (*Boogie theme. Cymbals. Black-Eyed Pea and Bubble run offstage and return immediately with a bowl of Stale Cake pieces. They scatter the cake about, leaving a trail going offstage, and they exit hurriedly. Ronn enters, sees the cake, and tastes it.*)

RONN

    Stale Cake! (*He whistles and waves. Garry and Steven run in to join him. They taste the cake.*)

ALL

    Stale Cake! Come on, you guys! (*Other children enter; all start yelling and run out, following the Stale Cake trail.*)

Scene xiii   The Stale Cake
Company at the Railway Station

A train whistle is heard. The members of the Stale Cake Company are standing about with their suitcases resting on the ground, as if waiting on a platform at a railway station. Diana Dumbstrut leans against the match, filing her nails. Daddy Tutti-Fruit Hat sits on his suitcase with his fake moustache pulled up on top of his head. He is picking his teeth. The Electric Piggybank Man, his pig mask pulled up, sits on his luggage between Diana Dumbstrut and Dorothy Doughie. Dorothy Doughie leans against the ladder, smoking. Captain Steal stands behind Dorothy Doughie, and the Oreo Cookie Man stands behind Diana Dumbstrut. Winde lies on the rim, observing everything.

DIANA DUMBSTRUT
   What time is it, huh? What time's it supposed to get here? Gee, I'm tired . . . kids've been steppin' all over my boots. Look . . . God, I hate kids.
OREO COOKIE MAN
   Yeah . . .
DOROTHY DOUGHIE
   How would you like 'em pullin' at your dress all the time, huh? You walk down the street and they tug at your dress. I want a Dorothy Doughie dress, I want a Dorothy Doughie doll! Oh God, teen pukes.
DADDY TUTTI-FRUIT HAT
   Hey, that's not a bad idea, sweetheart. A Dorothy Doughie doll, huh?
CAPTAIN STEAL
   Right on!
DADDY TUTTI-FRUIT HAT
   Dorothy and Don Doughie go camping. (*They ad-lib and laugh.*

157

Daddy Tutti-Fruit Hat looks at the Oreo Cookie Man.) You've got a little black paint behind your ear, Oreo.

DIANA DUMBSTRUT

Here, I'll get it.

CAPTAIN STEAL

Hey, Diana, do you think I can still pass for thirteen?

DIANA DUMBSTRUT

Sure, kid, you look young.

ELECTRIC PIGGYBANK MAN

We ain't takin' the Dream Wagon. Brakes busted.

DADDY TUTTI-FRUIT HAT

No sweat, Pig, no sweat. The Dream Wagon is junked.

OTHERS

What? Huh? Junked?

DADDY TUTTI-FRUIT HAT

Right! Now it's a spaceship.

OTHERS

Spaceship?

DADDY TUTTI-FRUIT HAT

Reworking the whole organization, see, I've got it all planned out. We're going to call it the Hot Carrot Juice Company. Oreo becomes a new logo! See now, we paint his face orange and give him some green hair and a carrot suit. Mr. Carrot Man! (*The members of the Stale Cake Company ad-lib comments and improvise bits to accompany this routine. Meanwhile Black-Eyed Pea and Bubble steal all the Big Money from their pockets and luggage and strew it across the stage, unseen by the Stale Cake Company. Daddy Tutti-Fruit Hat speaks to Diana Dumbstrut.*) I'll give you a carrot to twirl, sweetheart! You can twirl anything I put in your hand, can't you?

DIANA DUMBSTRUT

(*naively*) Hey, yeah, I could twirl a carrot!

DADDY TUTTI-FRUIT HAT

Peter Rabbit had a human sister, Miss Dorothy Patch! Captain Cabbage. Give me some green stuff, kids. Huh? We'll put some overalls on Pig, Mr. Pig Jeans. We're all set, huh? "Hot Carrot

Juice. Try some on your parents." All right, gimme an A . . . come on, let's try the song. (*The Stale Cake Company sings off-key in the background.*)

> *It's a carrot thing,*
> *It's an artichoke,*
> *It's a rutabaga . . .*

DIANA DUMBSTRUT

What is a rutabaga, anyway? Some kind of *root* or something?

DADDY TUTTI-FRUIT HAT

Oh, come on, I'm starved. Let's go get a Speedy Burger.

OREO COOKIE MAN

Yeah, a good Speedy Burger, huh.

CAPTAIN STEAL

I'm buying. (*He reaches into his pocket for his wallet.*) . . . I'm not buying, where's my money? (*Boogie theme. All begin searching frantically for their money, arguing among themselves and turning on the Electric Piggybank Man. All speak at once: "Where's my money?" "Pig, did you rip off the stash?" "It was right here by my . . ." "I ain't got the money!" "You can't trust anybody any more." The Oreo Cookie Man sees the money lying about; he whistles to the others.*)

OREO COOKIE MAN

It's the money! (*All start grabbing for the money, shouting. They follow the trail of money offstage. Both the trail of money and the trail of cake lead to the Matchbox House. As the lights black out and the Matchbox House slides onstage, Winde is heard singing from where he lies on the rim.*)

WINDE

> *Don't be grabbin' for more than you've got,*
> *Just know that you've got what you need!*
> *Don't be grabbin' for more than you've got,*
> *Just know that you've got what you need!*

Scene xiv   The Big Cookie

Winde, still lying on the rim, observes the Matchbox House people.
Wet Paint Bill and Old Glue Needle are working on umbrellas.
Mother Mary is by the stove, keeping an eye on the Big Cookie.

MOTHER MARY
The Big Cookie's getting brown. (*Black-Eyed Pea and Bubble come sliding in, talking excitedly. Wet Paint Bill and Old Glue Needle light large candles for themselves and Black-Eyed Pea.*)

BUBBLE
Mother Mary! Mother Mary! We found out what you meant in the song.

BLACK-EYED PEA
Yeah! Everybody's coming.

MOTHER MARY
You invited everybody?

BLACK-EYED PEA and BUBBLE
Yeah!

MOTHER MARY
And they're all coming?

BLACK-EYED PEA and BUBBLE
Yeah!

MOTHER MARY
That's fine! OK, get in your places now 'cause the Big Cookie's gonna be ready in just a minute. Quiet, though, because this is a holy moment. (*One by one, children and adults arrive at the Matchbox House. They enter quietly and gaze in awe at the house. A spirit of peace and love pervades the group. The children take seats around the stage and talk softly among themselves as Mother Mary greets the new arrivals.*) Hi! Come on in. Welcome to the Matchbox House. Welcome! Yes, yes, come in, come on in. Let me see how the cookie's doin'! Come on in, it'll be ready in a minute.

160

OLD GLUE NEEDLE

Just sit down and relax. The Big Cookie's comin' out in a minute.

MOTHER MARY

Here comes the Big Cookie! (*She pulls a huge cookie sheet from the oven; on it is an enormous cookie. Everyone "ooohs" and "aahs." They pass the cookie around, each breaking off a piece, sharing in the communion.*) Pass it on around! This ain't no stale cake either, just good fresh cookie.

SHEILA

How much?

MOTHER MARY

It's free. Here. I saw ya all on the street before, so you're welcome here at the Matchbox House.

BUBBLE

Hi, guys!

ALL

Hi, Bubble!

WET PAINT BILL

(*points to one boy*) I knew you'd be here. I saw your face in the street! Ha, ha, ha, ha!

BLACK-EYED PEA

I'll show you how to make that birdhouse tomorrow, all right?

BUBBLE

Have you seen my flute? I can teach you how to make one exactly like it.

BLACK-EYED PEA

You'll have to come back tomorrow. I know you like kittens, and I'll have some tomorrow. (*Percussion. The members of the Stale Cake Company enter down the slide one by one, each entrance accented by a rim shot on a drum in the orchestra. They gather in a clump upstage. They growl at the Cookie Land people, who growl back at them.*)

WET PAINT BILL

Oh, come on in, but don't you fret. Your cake may be stale, but ours ain't. (*The Stale Cake Company growls again, but the Matchbox House people growl back and frighten them.*)

DIANA DUMBSTRUT

Let's get out of here!

DOROTHY DOUGHIE

Help!

OREO COOKIE MAN

We gives up! We gives up!

DADDY TUTTI-FRUIT HAT

But we're trapped!

MOTHER MARY

Oh, no, folks, never mind. Everybody's welcome here in the Matchbox House. But only if you're joinin' in with us, only if you're sharin'.

DADDY TUTTI-FRUIT HAT

Oh, yeah? How much does it cost?

CAPTAIN STEAL

How much does it cost to join your club?

MOTHER MARY

No, no, no, not money! You don't pay to be filled with the spirit. You don't pay! You share in the spirit. You can't buy it, you gotta know it!

ELECTRIC PIGGYBANK MAN

We never took nothin' we didn't pay for!

OLD GLUE NEEDLE

That's 'cause you forgot the first recipe the good Lord ever gave ya.

WET PAINT BILL

You can't tell the difference between a piece of stale cake and a worn-out old shoe.

OLD GLUE NEEDLE

You probably never mixed a real recipe that makes a real cookie before in your life.

MOTHER MARY

You sell aprons, but I bet you never wore one and got it dirty in the kitchen. Here, taste this good fresh cookie. (*She gives the Stale Cake Company people some of the Big Cookie.*)

STALE CAKE COMPANY

Uhmmmmm! Uhmmmmm!

MOTHER MARY

Don't be greedy now! Now before you can join in and share, you got to do some work and make a real recipe, 'fore you can join us.

WET PAINT BILL

That's your penance for sellin' stuff nobody needs and gettin', gettin', gettin'! Take off that hair and all; it might fall in the mixing bowl and you know that ain't no good!

OLD GLUE NEEDLE

And all that stuff you're wearin' ain't no good neither!

MOTHER MARY

Now get goin' and do some good doin'. If you don't, you're goin' to be starvin', and whatever you do . . . (*gesturing for everyone to join her*) give, give, give! And remember, my friends . . .

MATCHBOX HOUSE PEOPLE

(*speaking one after another*) If you're cold! Hungry! Crabby! Frightened! Lost!

MOTHER MARY

You've just got to put it all together in one big bowl!

WET PAINT BILL

Now hurry up and get mixin'!

BLACK-EYED PEA

Get cookin'!

OLD GLUE NEEDLE

And get bakin'!

MOTHER MARY

The love in this here Matchbox House is yours for the takin'! (*The Stale Cake Company exits. Theme: "Put It All Together into One Big Bowl!"* Mother Mary sings.)

> *Oh, put it all together into one big bowl!*
> *Mix a new batch of cookies, now you been told!*
> *You'll never be hungry now in one big bowl!*
> *Put it all together into one big bowl!*

*Music on pages 172 and 173.

(Mother Mary sings the chorus, and the others onstage sing an echo-and-counterpoint.)

MOTHER MARY   ALL

You've got to put it . . .	*Put it!*
All together!	*'Gether!*
You've got to put it . . .	*Put it!*
All together!	*'Gether!*
You've got to put it . . .	*Put it!*
All together!	*All together!*
You've got to put it all to-	*Put — it — all —*
gether into one big bowl!	*in — one big bowl!*

(Mother Mary sings the next verse.)

> *Oh, put it all together into one big bowl!*
> *This recipe works for young and old!*
> *You're gonna get the spirit now in one big bowl!*
> *Put it all together into one big bowl!*

(Mother Mary and the others repeat the echo-and-counterpoint chorus as before. Then Mother Mary sings the next verse.)

> *Oh, put it all together into one big bowl!*
> *Pinch of yours, some of mine, you don't need gold!*
> *Guaranteed to taste delicious from one big bowl!*
> *Put it all together into one big bowl!*

(Mother Mary and the others repeat the chorus again. The members of the Stale Cake Company return without makeup or wigs, wearing chef suits and hats and carrying utensils. They set up a small table and mix a batch of dough as the others sing. Those who are seated get up, one by one, as the spirit builds; led by Black-Eyed Pea, they dance and sing down the center aisle, passing out cookies. The members of the Stale Cake Company follow the rest, passing out cookies and lemonade in tin cups. The audience is clapping and singing. The cast goes to the back of the house, around the sides, and back onto the stage for the finish of the song, urging people from the audience to join them. The house lights come up, and the people in the cast mix and visit with the people in the audience, again inviting them onto the stage. The spirit of communion pervades the final scene.)

The Cookie Jar. "And written in flour under the sink was this message: 'Bake a cookie for me!'" (Photograph by Gary Sherman.)

The Cookie Jar. "Black-Eyed Pea, Black-Eyed Pea, if you're wonderin' where this song comes from, then take a look at me!" (Photograph by Richard Paulaha.)

The Cookie Jar. "Miss Diana Dumbstrut, the Girl with the Golden Goose!"
(Photograph by Richard Paulaha.)

The Cookie Jar. "All right! We've got your number, sweetheart!"
(Photograph by Richard Paulaha.)

Sweet Jesus, Precious Savior

Black-Eyed Pea

NOTE: Music for *The Cookie Jar* composed by Roberta Carlson.
Copyright © 1974 by Roberta Carlson. All rights reserved.

Old Glue Needle and Wet Paint Bill

He's Old Glue Need-le, he's Wet-Paint Bill. If you need an-y-thing mend-ed, just ask us and we will be glad to do with a stitch and a dab, but you bet-ter let us fix you 'fore it gets too bad. Um-brel-las re-paired, Par-a-sols mend-ed! Let us get you back to where the Lord in-tend-ed, Um-brel-las re-paired, ten pen-nies if you will, done by Old Glue Need-le and Wet Paint Bill.

Get, Get, Get!

Moderato ~ Swing Tempo

Ya got-ta get, get, get; Ya got-ta get, get, get; When the

world's in trou-ble and you don't know what to do, ya got-ta get, get, get.

Put It All Together into One Big Bowl!

oh— Put it all to-geth-er in-to one big bowl, mix a

new batch of cook-ies now; you've been told you will

nev-er grow hun-gry now in one big bowl. Put it

all to - -geth-er in-to one big bowl. You've got to

Biographical Notes

Biographical Notes

JOHN CLARK DONAHUE is artistic director of the Children's Theatre Company of the Minneapolis Society of Fine Arts. He is also an associate director of the Minneapolis Institute of Arts and serves as the Region V Governor of the Children's Theatre Association.

Donahue has written and directed the following plays for the Children's Theatre Company: *Good Morning, Mister Tillie; Hang On to Your Head; Variations on a Similar Theme — An Homage to René Magritte; Old Kieg of Malfi; How Could You Tell?; A Wall; The Cookie Jar; The Sitwells at Sea* (in collaboration with Gar Hildenbrand); and *The Netting of the Troupial.* In addition, Donahue wrote the libretto for Dominick Argento's opera *A Postcard from Morocco* and directed the Minnesota Opera Company's production of the opera in 1971. He also wrote and directed *A Suitcase,* a play that was filmed in color by the Children's Theatre Company in 1974.

Donahue received the 1973 Arts Council Award for his outstanding contribution to the arts in Minnesota, and in 1974 he was recognized as Arts Administrator of the Year by *Arts Management,* a trade publication addressing itself to innovative management in all the arts throughout the United States.

LINDA WALSH JENKINS is currently a Danforth Graduate Fellow in the theater arts doctoral program at the University of Minnesota. She

177

was literary editor of the Children's Theatre Company when the scripts of the plays in this volume were first assembled; later she prepared the manuscripts of the plays and related materials for publication.

Jenkins's theater experience includes acting with the Rice Players (Rice University) and study at the Dallas Theater Center and the University of Minnesota. She taught acting at the University of Minnesota and performed with the Anyplace Theater of Minneapolis before joining the Children's Theatre Company in 1969 as secretary-actress and subsequently as literary editor.

ROBERTA CARLSON is a professional composer, arranger, and jazz pianist. She has composed scores for the Children's Theatre Company since 1965; she joined the staff as music director in 1969.

Carlson's compositions for the Children's Theatre Company include scores for *Old Kieg of Malfi, How Could You Tell?, The Legend of Sleepy Hollow, Kidnapped in London, Jerusalem, Sleeping Beauty,* and *The Cookie Jar.* She also composed scores for *Fables Here and Then, An Italian Straw Hat, The Miracle Man,* and *Bull Moose.*